Asatru

Learning About Norse Mythology and Poetic Edda

(The Complete Guide to Heathenry Paganism, Gods and Cosmology)

Carolyn Norris

Published By **Zoe Lawson**

Carolyn Norris

Asatru: Learning About Norse Mythology and Poetic Edda (The Complete Guide to Heathenry Paganism, Gods and Cosmology)

ISBN 978-1-998901-71-5

Legal & Disclaimer

Table of Contents

Chapter 1: What Is Asatru?

Asatru refers to the title that is given to the religious beliefs embraced by the early Nordic Neo-pagan cultures that lived prior to Christianity. Asatru is believed to refer to "to be true to the Aesir," who were the collective of Norse gods, who were featured in Norse mythology. The word Asatru was not used at the time, but it was adopted in the 19th century to refer to the practice of worshiping Norse gods as well as the pagan religion that went through an upsurge.

The most wealthy members of society during the 19th century began to become fascinated by archaeology, and they funded some of the most extensive excavations of the period. The fascination with the past and the various religions grew as the rise of industrialization led to people were more involved in their ancestral roots and forgotten customs. They found the modern age and the transformations that it was experiencing to be fast-paced and required them to go back to their ancestral place and time when traditional practices were less stress-inducing than the modern industrialization.

European civilizations were influenced by nature and adopted all religions and civilizations that were based on the seasonal cycle of life and living off the landscape. Prior to the war in 1914 they were a part of the continent, but were scattered and unorganized. It was only in the 1970s when groups of people from

Iceland and in the United Kingdom, and the US joined to form more organized groups that reflected the customs that were followed by Nordic as well as Germanic people, as well as the Anglo Saxons from the UK.

They became the early precursors of the Asatru movement that continues to expand and attract more followers each year. The initial groups were given names such as those of the Viking Brotherhood in the US and the Asatru Folk Alliance in the UK. There were other associations that soon came up and adopted names such as Vanatru or the Rite of Odin but continued to come up with new concepts and theories about what they believed to be the Old Ways and the Norse pagan practices.

Certain followers were associated with some followers identified with Vikings They also believed in Asatru. Asatru was referred to as the faith of the Viking period, but it also adopted pagan traditions that were prevalent in central Europe. The Vikings are the first time we have heard of Scandinavia in the books of history and, though being an Viking was a job however, it was incorporated as a name to define the society of the time. Archaeology of the Viking period revealed that the rituals and customs of the time could be utilized in contemporary cultures to bring people together and teach them how to be in harmony with nature and live a more prosperous life.

The cultural representations found in JRR Tolkien books further reignited the fascination with Asatru and the Marvel franchise further emphasized this. Norse stories and myths contain fantastic tales of heroic heroes and powerful characters, however they also depict gods' faults and errors. These gods and goddesses from

Norse mythology are depicted as beings with human-like personalities. They are seen as beings who reside among us, not being gods that should be worshiped. There is no bowing to Norse gods, they speak with them and seek their advice. The gods receive sacrifices and gifts to honor and show respect however, they are gods who are associated with the natural world and human attributes, not heavenly beings.

The practice of religion and Asatru introduced magic and gods into the lives of its adherents. Nature and magic became the norm for living and celebrating the seasons was an easy way to mark the passing of the years. The Pagans as well as Nordic people relied on Asatru as a guide to teach them an honorable and respectful lifestyle so that they could be satisfied with their life on earth and ascend to the heavens with no regrets. This is a belief that still can be a model for the ideal life that we all should strive to.

How the Asatru Is Organized

The Gothar

The Asatru's members Asatru are known as Kindred and are described as Heathens and don't adhere to any strict doctrines or rules however they have their own priesthood referred to under the title of the Gothar which refers to the plural form of this phrase Gothi as well as Gythia. In the past the Gothar formed a group of people that formed The Godic Republic as well as being accountable for the administration of the population. They also founded Hofs and temples where the followers could commune with gods and give them gifts.

In the modern world the Gothar are as significant. They are charged with reviving ancient ways of living Old Ways and teaching the Kindred how to connect to the soul of the ancient Norse and purify it by eliminating all Christian beliefs. A successful Gothar is similar to warriors and draws strength from the gods of war, Thor, Odin, and the devotion of Freya, the goddess. Freya. Some people will not be able to achieve this level however those who achieve it will have demonstrated their worth as members of their position in the Asatru community. While everyone in the Kindred is able to perform private rituals at home or with their family Only the Gothar can lead sacred events to the community.

The Asatru is growing in its numbers and is among the fastest-growing religion in Iceland. The number of people who join increases each year, and is increasing across the world. Icelandic Association Icelandic association is run by the chief

Gothi along with nine others Gothar who cover the geographic regions. The meetings are held weekly and are open to all and deal with matters like weddings, naming ceremonies, and funerals. The meetings draw lots of interest and is highly loved by the general public.

They commemorate the four major seasons with extravagant celebrations and feasts to celebrate the goddesses, gods, and the happiness to be Asatru. They don't speak or conduct any sort of missionary work in order to convince others to join them; they don't have to. In a culture which has become disenchanted with formal religions the freedom that comes with Asatru is appealing to all.

In Reykjavik the first pagan temple constructed in more than 1,000 years was constructed in the year 2018 to accommodate the growing number of visitors to their celebrations and meetings.

The building was shut down during the beginning stages to stop the construction and to bless Mother Nature for her timber that was used to construct this new building. It's not something you'll often see, but a holy moment where you witness the Old Ways are combined with modern construction techniques and the results are both practical as well as spiritual.

Asatru isn't just about values and beliefs it advocates. The members are encouraged to actively discredit groups that adhere to the religion under the banner of war, violence as well as intolerance, racism and violence. They follow"the "Viking way" by exploiting extreme versions of Norse practices and naming them Asatru. They are neo-Nazis have joined with Asatru and have claimed to be as the Aryan Nation. The truth is that Asatru beliefs are completely contradiction to what they believe in and any association is false and misrepresents the religion.

It is reported that the Icelandic branch has been hit with threats and hate mail because of their position on topics like gay marriages as well as human rights. They have been steadfast in their fight for equality for all people and have been stung by the results. Despite all efforts to dissuade them, they frequently have hundreds of marriages that are same-sex that are officiated by the Gothar which means that couples come from all over of the world to participate.

Anyone can participate in Asatru as well as join groups across the globe However, the Icelandic branch is only open to members who are fully enrolled in their own country. If you are brought up in Iceland or reside in the country, you're eligible to jointhe group, and there are no conditions to membership. The race, sexual orientation and ethnicity are not relevant as the group is open to anyone.

Here are a few of the most popular companies:

The Troth

The Troth is an international group committed to the heathen as well as Asatru practices. They strive to inform their followers and offer information and training to make them more aware of the traditional practices and Northern European religions, cultures and their heritage. They are a follower of their gods, the Norse Gods, the gods of Aesir as well as the Vanir which includes Odin, Freya, and Thor.

Their programs of training are designed to offer members the opportunity to be stewards of their respective areas and impart the knowledge of Asatru to the residents of that area. They're not missionaries and their job isn't to make converts, but they're educated to become scholars and provide examples of how to live a moral lifestyle that is based on values of Asatru and Norse heathenry.

The Asatru Alliance

Asatru Alliance Asatru Alliance is based in Payson, Arizona but has branches throughout the world. They greet their friends by saying "Welcome Home" and provide an organization that is non-profit and designed to unite followers and offer them a platform to learn and research about everything that is related to Asatru.

There's a full listing of Alliance Kindreds where you can examine your local area and determine if there's any local groups that you could join. Some groups are already in place to host Asatru Althing meetings, and those who have submitted an application for a permit have the full right to vote. Althing is a conference named in honor of the Icelandic parliament, where members are able to discuss their grievances and suggest ways for the group to be improved, and is scheduled every year. All Kindreds are required to attend, either in person or via proxy The majority of the members vote for the hosts at the Althing. These meetings are designed to ensure efficient running of the Alliance and allow an equal opportunity for everyone to hear.

Irminsul Aettir

This site is comprehensive that provides information on groups throughout the globe. The map of contact details includes information of groups in Europe, the USA, Canada, Europe as well as the rest of the world. There are a myriad of groups that are located in some of the most bizarre places. From the folk from Asatru Argentina and the kindred of the Wolven

Spear in Scotland There are a variety of ways to connect with fellow Asatru fans and to share passions. This site is particularly fascinating for those who are new to the Asatru religion. There are organized groups of like-minded those who are interested in the ancient ways, and are brimming with enthusiasm for the Asatru faith as well as the Norse gods.

These are just a few of the quotes on the site:

Ben an sniper located in the Kiwi Barracks in Salisbury, England, writes, "The amount of death I have encountered during two tours of Iraq has made me question my faith in formal religions. I am a simple warrior who would like to practice blots and symbels with other like-minded warriors and maidens. I accept that the allfather has fated me to Valhalla and would like to begin preparations for my fate."

Alexander of Ukraine writes "My ancestor is a Germanic god from the Amelung dynasty, and my surname is gapt which is a corrupted form of gaut, the name of Odin. Does this mean I am related to him?"

Tasha of Moscow simply says, "I am a pagan Buddhist who worships Loki."

Irminsul Aettir Irminsul Aettir is a voluntary organization that promotes sharing of information and resources. It is filled with helpful articles. They claim that they seek to collaborate to promote Asatru and promote an organized and flexible style of worship.

The International Asatru Foundation

The organization on Facebook is dedicated to the practice and practiced of the heathen religion among anyone in the globe. The group is over 4000 people and hold live sessions of questions and answers with those who are members from the religion. They also host a weekly show called called Odin's Eye, is full of information and facts regarding the foundation and its operations.

They're committed to research into the past and serve as the basis to Germanic paganism and ethics-based work.

Northvegr Organization

This site is intended ideal for serious academics and scholars who wish to learn more about Northern practices and the long-standing practices they practiced. They offer a wealth of information covering the role of shield maidens, as well as the practice of pre-Christian heathen rituals that were practiced in the North.

Asatru is about making choices The organizations that Asatru is associated with offer an opportunity to become part of a larger group or remain an individual member, however with greater understanding. Because of the modern means of communication, you are able to connect with Asatru followers across the globe. Asatru is all about creating a better world by encourages people to join forces in order to accomplish this. Utilize these resources and links to learn more about the meaning of Asatru is to people from different cultural backgrounds. Do you have the same beliefs that those of Russia and Brazil? Learn more by asking questions; you might be amazed by the results.

Global divisions are possible to overcome in addition, Asatru may be the path forward to bring the world closer. Peace, unity and cohesion can be expand and bring people on earth in harmony and love. Join the cause and utilize Asatru for your shared link to join and build bonds.

Chapter 2: Norse Gods

The Norse Gods were an interesting group, and they were not without conflict with each with each other. Many people have heard of the big names like Odin, Loki, and Thor through their media representations as well as because they are featured in many of the popular tales of the time. They'll be here, however, also others less well-known names, with stories which are equally fascinating and offer entertainment as well as the principles that make up the religious system of Asatru.

Baldur

Baldur was the son of Odin Baldur, the son of Odin and Frigg, Baldur was the most attractive of all the Gods and was loved by all because of his joy and enthusiasm for life. When he began having thoughts of his own demise and he told the mother of his that he was worried for his lying and she went to every living thing in Midgard which was the place of the living and made them swear to swear to never hurt their beloved son.

The gods of other gods were fascinated by his immunity and randomly toss weapons and other deadly objects at him to test his strength. Loki was fascinated and inquired of Frigg if she'd not asked any of the living creatures to swear to. She informed him that she had not bothered to inquire about the mistletoe as they were small and insignificant. They were the least likely plant to hurt her son. Loki quickly fashioned the spear out of mistletoe and got the god of blind warriors Hodr to launch it towards Baldur during a meal. The spear delivered its fatal message and Baldur was killed.

The gods of other gods were unhappy about the death of Baldur that they set up an assembly to determine how to reverse the action of Loki and they decided to send Baldur's brother must go to Hel god of death to help his brother. Hermod swiftly climbed Odin's eight-legged horse to make the treacherous trip into the underworld, where the brother he was looking for was with a ragged and battered appearance sitting beside goddess Hel. He persuaded the goddess let him go and she agreed to the terms , ensuring that all creatures on earth would be able to mourn the loss of his brother.

Everyone agreed and shed tears for Baldur However, Loki was once again in the way. It disguised itself as the giantess dubbed Thokk and did not cry, saying that Baldur was never anything positive for his character. The incident sealed Baldur's fate and he was relegated to Hel until the incident of Ragnarok. Loki fled into the mountains, surrounded by the vengeful goddesses and gods. Loki was finally spotted by the all-seeing eyes of Odin and was transformed into a fish to escape.

Loki leapt, squirmed in the form of a salmon, and then attempted to swim upriver in order to reach the ocean. The attempt was thwarted by the God of Thunder Thor who grabbed Loki with his tail, and dragged Loki from the river. The reason for Loki's grip is for the reason that the salmon has such an elongated tail.

In his former appearance, Loki was taken to the cave and rescued by Odin. Two of his sons were already in the cave but Odin changed one into a wolf. The wolf was then violently devoured by his brother while Loki watched in awe. The innards were used to create chains that bind Loki to the rock formations of the cave. A serpent was hung over his head. The venom would fall down on Loki and make him shake to the point that it could cause shaking in Midgard.

Loki's wife was close by and tried to take the venom to save her husband from pain But they both knew that they'd be there until the event of Ragnarok.

Bragi

God of Poetry and elegance. He is a child of Odin and Frigg and had runes engraved on his tongue. He was a great inspiration to humans to write poetry by inviting them to drink from a mead cup and poetry. The cup also served to celebrate the death of a monarch, and the new monarch would drink it prior to taking over the throne.

Forseti

A son to Baldur and Nanna Baldur God of reconciliation and justice. The gods and the humans accepted his rulings, and no one was left without the option of deciding. He established Norse laws that everyone were able to follow and respect, and his rulings were the final decision. In contrast to his elder counterparts who relied on more violence to repress their enemies and punishment, he is believed to be as one of the gods younger who preferred to settle disputes peacefully.

Freyr

It is believed that the Norse God of Fertility, Freyr was the son of god of the sea, Njord. He was at first considered a Vanir but was later accepted by the Aesir when peace reigned over the worlds of nine. He was a resident of the palace of Alfheim and was regarded as one among the strongest gods during the Viking period. He is a gentle beautiful and loving god of sunlight and solar energy and his name is Lord.

He travels through the sky aboard a mythical ship called Skidbladnir that is so massive it could accommodate all gods, yet was so magical after he had used it that he was able to fold it down so small that it can fit in a pocket. Freyr flew through the sky with his boar and his bristles sparkled in the sun , and brought illumination to Midgard.

The most well-known story of Freyr is one about love. Freyr was on his way towards the seat of Odin which allowed him to view all the worlds. He also spotted the woman of his dreams. Freyr was completely enthralled and declared himself deeply in love with the girl whom he later learned was Gerd who is the child of an enormous called Jotun. The love he felt was so intense that Freyr was unable to eat , and became sick when he became more enthralled with Gerd and the ways to win her love.

The father was so concerned about his son, the servant was sent to discover why the boy was acting so bizarrely. The servant informed him that Freyr was in love with Freyr and was in love with her, so Njord ordered the servant to on a trip to Jotun to bring Gerd back to the Jotun to wed his son. The servant was gifted Freyr's magic sword in order to protect him,

The servant soon spotted Gerd and offered her a number of presents to get married Freyr however, the giantess didn't have any. The woman was furious and turned down further offers and gifts until the servant was so angry in his anger that he offered to curse Gerd along with her relatives. The threats were so potent they convinced Ged to get married to Freyr and after waiting for nine days the couple finally received his wish and they were married.

Loki

The god of tricks is one of the gods with the highest amount of documentation from Norse mythology. He was among the first anti-heroes from time and gained fame for his tricks, but also became known as a mean god in the later years.

The first of his acts was to give advice to gods about how to be able to get Asgard constructed without massive costs. They had already constructed the city, but did not have the money to build the wall of protection to protect the city's gods. They employed a giant with a massive stallion called Svadilfari who threw massive boulders night and day. Loki had made a promise to the gods that the giant that he would never complete the wall, therefore they decided to give him sun, moon, as well as the goddess Freya after the project was completed. They became anxious as they realized the impossibly difficult task would be completed as well as the monster would demand payment, so they contacted Loki for help.

Loki transformed into a gorgeous mare that attracted the giant's stallion to marry her. The stallion was so excited by his new lover that work on the wall stopped and the giant was unable to complete the task. Loki who was still as a mare was pregnant with the eight-legged colt called Sleipnir and was to become Odin's most trusted horse.

Loki, Odin, and his son Thor became fast-paced friends, and they embarked upon unforgettable adventures. Odin was the most powerful, Loki the mischief-maker, and Thor the muscle. They may not share blood, but they're the blood siblings who taken vows to defend each other.

Loki was a lover of women and had relationships with numerous goddesses. The couple was Angrboda and had a son named Fenrir, the giant wolf that is infamous within Norse mythology, as the spawner of chaos and destruction. They also had Jormungand who was the Midgard serpent that ruled the world of visible light, as well as Hel, goddess of death.

The second woman he married, Sigyn, bore him two sons: Narvi and Vali and Vali, who were both present at the cave as Loki was locked for the last time. Vali changed into a beast and devoured his dear sister, Narvi.

Njord

God from the ocean. When he wed to Skadi Their union was sworn in by a dramatic moment that took place in Norse history. In Asgard gods and goddesses kept young thanks to goddess Idunn who was the guardian of the fruit of youth. If they noticed signs of age then they ate one of her magical apple and instantly changed into youthful beings.

One day , the giant of frost known as Thiassi was captured by Loki and had agreed to let him go in exchange for Loki assisted in capturing Idunn and get those magical fruits. Loki was willing to help the giant take the goddess away. The gods immediately felt the effects and began to age quickly. They became weaker and started to lose their strength. Odin was furious at Loki's actions, and threatened Loki by threatening him with the cold curse if he did not bring back Idunn to her proper spot in Asgard.

Loki became a falcon before flying into the realm of giants, and there he met the goddess. He transformed to a walnut in order to transport him back Asgard. Thiassi was furious and decided to chase Loki and get his captor back. He transformed himself into a powerful eagle and began to chase Loki. The gods saw Thiassi and created a massive fire to slow his speed. Thiassi was thrown into the flames, and was consumed by the flames. Odin took his eyes, and then tossed them in the sky, forming new stars. Idunn went back to her magical orchard.

Skadi was the son of Thiassi and was seeking compensation for the death of her father. They promised her a divine to be her spouse, but was only permitted to see their feet in order to make her decision. She picked the most gorgeous feet she could see she believed they belonged to Baldur however was shocked to discover that they actually were the property of Njord. The seawater kept his feet looking young and beautiful. The wedding was a success however Skadi was unhappy because she was dedicated to the mountains, while her husband was a devotee of the sea.

They were at the mountain, during which Njord was awakened by the cries of wolves. She was also averse to the cold, chilly air. Then, they spent nine days near the ocean, where Skadi complained that she was kept awake, this time, by seagulls. The couple realized that they could not be together in any location So they made the decision to leave and return home alone, to their beloved homes.

Odin

The godfather is among the most complex and mysterious characters that are found in Norse mythology. He is connected to war, wisdom poetry, death royalty, runesand sorcery, and various other spiritual beliefs. He is the father of Borr and Bestla and was married to Frigg who is called Freya. He has fathered numerous children and forged many different branches of royalty.

Odin and his brothers Vili as well as Ve killed Ymir the giant of frost who was the ruler of the first days and utilized his blood, flesh and bones to form the universe. Ymir was believed to be the first human to be born and is believed to be to be the father of all the ice giants. Odin created the Earth out of his body and his blood shaped the oceans and rivers. The brothers then utilized his skull to construct the sky, and then added molten rock to form stars. the brains of Ymir were put into the sky to create clouds. Since Earth was flat they made use of the eyebrows of Ymir and his lashes to create mountains and barriers.

The brothers found two pieces of wood on the beach and breathed the life of the first human beings. The two human beings then got married and had a couple of beautiful children, named Sol Moon and Sol. Moon. They believed these children were beautiful and mysterious for world, and so enslaved their souls and released them into the heavens. Sol was gifted a fast car that she rides across the sky, and is chased by a fierce predator, while her brother follows the same route but less speed.

The brothers realized that the earth should become connected with the sky by constructing a rainbow bridge. The perfect rainbow is a sign of its connection to God since humans cannot make such an amazing product.

Odin is the ruler of Valhalla Odin is the ruler of Valhalla, the Norse home of the dead for warriors. It is also the most revered place where humans could reside after death. He was the ruler of the Valkyries and brought together the most skilled warriors of their kingdom in preparation for fights of Ragnarok. Odin is considered to be one of the most important forces of Norse religions, and is an expert in wisdom, knowledge and understanding.

Odin sacrificed himself in order to acquire more knowledge and is depicted as a god who has only one eye, with only one socket. He offered this eye over to the Mimir's Well of Wisdom in exchange for the chance to drink the magical waters of the well. He went through a lot of hardship and suffering to catch an idea at the magical power and comprehend the meaning behind the runes. His nine-day trial involved cutting himself in the back and then being hanged by the branch of Yggdrasil. His eye sacrificed to Odin is placed in the hands of the talking head, and gives Odin the ability to see into the future and further away.

Thor

Due to the popularity of the media's popularity, Thor is one of the most well-known characters in Norse mythology. Thor was the god of thunder, who is a part of Asgard in the Asgard region and serves as the most feared defender of the gods and goddesses of other gods. He is the focus of numerous stories and is frequently portrayed as a hero, however his image isn't always in a positive manner.

One of Thor's strongest weapons is Mjolnir his powerful hammer One time, the Thor of his dreams was horrified to discover that an enormous ice monster named

Thrym had snatched his hammer and held it for ransom until the gods let him marry Freyja. Freyja was opposed to the union and pleaded with Loki to find a different solution to the problem. He joined forces with Thor and came up with a solution.

Thor is convinced by Thor to wear drag and act as The goddess Freyja while Loki dressed as her handmaid. They arrive at the Hall of Thrym The two returned the hammer to them which they used to destroy the giant and his companions.

Thor is often seen as a god of power, however lacking the wisdom of his father. He was often beaten down by Loki and made to appear silly, yet he nevertheless valued for his courage and honour. Thor was the standard jock, with an innate heart.

Tyr

Tyr is most well-known for his role as the God of War, however there's more to his duties. Tyr is also the god of justice and retribution. This connection offers us an understanding of how Vikings and Norsemen believed. They believed that war, justice law and retribution were the same thing and that battles in the field of war were equally important as battles in the courtroom. Odin is the god responsible for making battle plans, while Tyr is the God of rules that governed those battles.

The most well-known story of Tyr tells of the fierce wild wolf Fenrir. As a wolf was a puppy The gods quickly discovered that he was powerful and growing in size. They were afraid that he'd take on all of them and take them all down, so they surrounded the wolf with chains. Fenrir was aware that the gods were trying to fool him and take him hostage, which is why he consented to being chained if one of them placed his arm into the mouth of a wolf as a symbol of confidence.

The gods were all too scared of the consequences to extend their hands, but Tyr recognized that someone needed to stand up for themselves. He put his arm into Fenrir's mouth and allowed gods to put chains around the neck of the wolf. Fenrir was so enraged by the rick that he ripped Tyr's arm in protest. The sacrifice performed by Tyr signified that the gods were secure again however, Fenrir's selfless act is motivated by his instinctive sense of justice, which is why Fenrir is always looking for revenge. Certain prophecies suggest that the revenge of Tyr will take place in Ragnarok.

Ull

The god of shooting, skiing and also being a skilled warrior Ull is a mysterious persona that isn't well-known as a part of

Norse time. He is regarded as"the patron saint for skiers", and was famous for his athleticism, strength and athleticism. The Eddas only contain a handful of references to his name in the Eddas however he is still seen as an important persona. There are numerous locations within the Nordic counties bearing his name. Ull as well as Ullr in the region's name suggest that at some time the inhabitants there constructed temples for the mysterious god.

The god may not have been mentioned in the works in Edda the Poetic Edda, but Odin made reference to him in the expression "Ull and all his gods," which indicated that the idea that he had of Ull as the god of all time. In a different Nordic text, the mention of swearing oaths on Ull's ring is a reference to the most important swearing you will ever make.

According to some historians, Ull became the ruler of the gods of other gods after Odin was banished. He remained the god over the gods till Odin was reinstated to his former position.

Chapter 3: Norse Goddesses

The gods of Asatru are a formidable group however, back when women were kings, they also had their own. Female warriors faced off with the same courage power, strength, and determination as their male counterparts in battle. Female warriors and shield maidens took on the same battles as their male counterparts and among the most well-known women in the Viking epics is Lagertha she was her spouse Ragnar Lodbrok.

Even women who had been left behind were the fierce guardians of their farms. Their husbands would leave for months and it was up to the women to keep their family safe, and to grow crops and produce food to live. The conditions and weather they had to contend with made them hardy and would fight with a hammer and a sledgehammer to protect their families. They developed their character traits inspired by the goddesses depicted in Norse epics that instilled them and led by their example.

Eir

The goddess of healing Eir can be found in both the Aesir clan as well as the Valkyries and her responsibilities included selecting warriors who could survive the fights. She is a major element of Norse mythology, and was revered by warriors and their families because she was the one who held their lives in her own hands. Her healing abilities give us an understanding of the Scandinavian lifestyle and where women were the most effective healers.

Eostre

Eostre is the god of spring. Festival Ostara is celebrated in her honour. She's not featured in many epics however she is a symbol of the dawn of new eras as well as the moment of efficiency. She dances with life to celebrate spring. She is often seen as a young girl wearing flowers on her head.

Elli

One of the lesser-known goddesses, Elli is the goddess of ageing and, in one Norse epic, she is featured along with Loki as well as Thor. Thor, the god of thunder, was in a journey together with Loki and had to face many obstacles. He was already beaten by a drink contest but is now determined to make sure he gets to a point. He tells the crowd that he would like to fight an opponent and challenge the crowd to a match.

The giant who was in charge of their halls, was adamant about asking Thor to take on his former nurses, Elli. Thor was shocked to see an elderly lady stumble through the doorway, and was amazed that his opponent appeared so weak. The match began and Thor held onto the lady who was stricken however she remained steadfast. She grasped Thor and the huge warrior was forced to kneel. The fight continued followed, and Thor was thrown to the ground. The giant intervened, declaring Elli the winner which was a shock to Thor.

Freyja

Freyja is the god of beauty, love sexuality, magic, and death. Her twin is Freyr as well as her dad is Njord, the god of the sea. She is a resident of the mansion known as Folkvangr where the majority of the dead Vikings would be a part of her. She will be the first option of dead warriors, while the rest would reside together with Odin as well as the Valkyries.

Freyja is the strongest and most revered goddess. She was also the lover who was a master of the art of sedr. It is the ability to alter the course of your destiny, and to cast spells to bring luck or curses for the person who was affected.

The husband of her Od disappeared, and stories were told about her gold-colored tears when she longingly longed for her husband who was no longer there However, she was reported to be unfaithful to Od. Freyja had the power of beauty as well as love and was considered to be the most beautiful of the goddesses. She rode a chariot steered by cats through the skies and was adorned with a cloak made of falcon feathers which let her fly swiftly into the realm where the giants resided. She was extremely gracious with her feathers, and often gave it to other gods in order to move swiftly.

Freyja was a fan of jewelry and came to an unexpected arrangement with a group of Dwarves to have a gorgeous necklace called Brisingamen. She was out for an outing and discovered an underground cave, and saw four dwarves working on most exquisite piece of jewelry she's ever seen. Freyja wanted it, so she inquired of the dwarves what amount of gold would be needed to purchase the piece. They refused to listen, but they came up with a plan.

They explained to Goddess that they could only ensure to have this necklace would be to stay up late with the dwarves, making love all night long. She agreed, and then for the next four days, she stayed together with the crafters of the dwarfs inside the cave. When the time was right to leave, she quit the cave came back home like nothing had ever happened.

Frigg, Who Is Also Known as Frigga

The wife of god Odin Frigg, she is also the mom of Aesir and is beloved by everyone. Her abilities include regulating conditions of the earth, helping ensure order and peace in the skies as well as creating a soothing atmosphere. She's more than an adornment to Odin and is frequently portrayed with him as an equal partner, and as a wise and nurturing partner. She ruled Asgard with female power and promoted fertility and motherhood both in mortals and humans.

She outwitted her husband as they were settling a dispute between the two tribes: the Vandals and Winnilers. Odin stated that he would select the winner based on which tribe he observed the next morning from his window at home. Frigg convinced women from The Winniler tribe to have their hair appear like beards, and then stand in front of Odin's window. After seeing the ladies, Odin declared the Winnilers were the winners. He later discovered his wife's tricks, but was able to decide she was right to aid the

Winnilers because it was obvious that they would win. This proved he was respectful of his wife's views.

Gefjun

The goddess of agriculture as well as fertility. She was the goddess who married an enormous and mortal King. The name of the giant isn't known however, she was said to have four sons and her wedding to the King of Denmark resulted in her living an ordinary life living in Lejre for a long time.

She is known by the name of goddess plowing and her story is a cult within Norse mythology. She was wandering around Sweden disguised as an homeless old crone, when she came across the King of Sweden who was a generous and generous fellow. He assured her that she would be able to cultivate some land however, her skills at plowing will decide it. He assured her that any farmland she could plough using four oxen over a entire day would be hers. The present was already generous however Gefjun was looking for more. She called her four enormous sons and made them gigantic Oxen. They were hard at work and ploughed the vast area as well as dragged away the vast parcel of land and pulled far away from Sweden. The hole they left filled with water and is the location of Lake Marlaren, while the land they took turned into Zealand which is the Danish Island which is now the location of Copenhagen, the capital of Denmark. Danish capital city of Copenhagen.

Hel

Death goddess, and the the daughter of Loki. She was a resident of Helheim and was ejected from the city by Odin due to her appearance so unattractive that she irritated his eyes. Her realm is the most dark of the kingdoms in Norse mythology, and is also the burial place for souls that have been slain. The process of dying was one of the most important aspects of Norse tradition and those who perished in battle on foreign soils were considered to be the most noble death, whereas those who died on their home on their own soil, fighting for their land were considered less reverent. The death of old age or disease was not the best option for dying and could mean that the person ended being buried in the company of Hel the dark kingdom.

It is said that her appearance can be described as half beautiful and half grotesque. Her face looks as her father's, but the other half of her body is scruffy and angry, similar to her massive mother. The top part of her body is similar to normal females, while the bottom part has decaying skin and swollen legs. Her skin is always disappearing from her body and her expression is brutal but half dead. The media describes her as harsh and cruel to other people and shows no concern for the destiny of other people.

Idun

The apple keeper of youth. Her magical apple made her among the best adored goddesses of the heavens as well as being associated with sexuality and eroticism.

Jord

The goddess of the giant has the title of mother to Thor however, she's not featured in numerous Norse stories. Her name is derived from the word earth and her role as the mother of Thor is believed to be her most prominent duty.

Nerthus

This goddess with holy power is more closely associated with Germanic time than Norse. Her connection to the earth is powerful and she has an esoteric grove, where holy women and men could visit her, and her cart, drawn by bulls. At times, she travels through the lands and is welcomed by celebrations and love. Anywhere she travels, she has been blessed by peacefulness and there is no need to leave or be at war.

Nott

The goddess of dream and night. Her father is huge and her mother is unidentified. She was married three times and had a child from each marriage named Aud which means money, Dagr, meaning day and her third child was Jord The goddess who represented earth. Nott is the personification of the night and is a dark , eerie figure hidden in mystery. She symbolizes the bliss of sleeping, when we are able to let go of our worries and let the burdens of life go away while we rest. Her ability is to convince that you let go of the burden and relax. Nott will also invoke the divine feeling of emptiness, the feeling that you experience in frightening places , and that feeling of anxiety when you're unsure about your security.

Ran

Goddess of the Sea dwells deep in the sea together with her husband Aegir. They reign over the seas along and their 9 daughters, and enjoy a harmonious relation with heaven. Ran would sit beneath the waves, with her huge fishing net in anticipation of passing ships. She would throw her net to bring them to their watery deaths to spend all their time in her company and with the family she raised. Since the Vikings spent all their time in the seas, they practiced specific rituals to honor Ran to ensure they avoided drowning.

Sif

Thor's wife is usually depicted sporting long golden hair and a beautiful face. The woman is often mentioned in texts from the past however, the mentions are primarily attributed to their husbands, kids and gorgeous hair. Her most significant part was to create the powerful Hammer of Thor. The god of tricks Loki chooses to chop off Sif's gorgeous hair, which leaves her shocked and her husband furious.

Thor threats to kill Loki in the event that he doesn't find an even more stunning hairstyle in his wife's hair, however there isn't any natural hair with the beauty of Sif's locks. He decided to ask the dwarfs for help in creating the headpiece made of gold that would be placed on top of Sif's head to replace her hair with gold. As the dwarfs worked and were so enthralled that they came up with the famous Hammer of Thor named Mjolnir. It was a blessing for Sif they also designed an amazing headpiece. stunning that she was filled with joy when she saw returning to her gold locks.

Sigyn

Sigyn is Loki's wife , and the mother of Loki's two sons. She was there by his side during the time Loki was thrown into an eternal cave. She is the epitome of loyalty and standing by your loved loved ones, regardless of the circumstances.

Skadi

Skadi is the Norse goddess of winter, snow and skiing. Skadi is located in the top of mountains where snow doesn't melt. Her halls are referred to as Thrymheim as they were described by god Odin in the form of"the "court of the ancients." Although Skadi is a giganticess she is more light and compassionate than her fellow race. She was referred to as the shining bride of the gods. She symbolizes strength and power and her bravery and endurance are well-known. Her name is "harm in the shadows" and is used to refer to Scandinavia which is a reference into Skadi's Isle.

Sol

One of the goddesses of the beginning, Sol is the goddess of the sun as well as all solar power. In Norway the sun is able to shine for two months at the same time. Sol was revered and numerous temples were constructed in her honour. Sol can be seen flying through the sky along with two of her horses being pursued by the god of the wolf, Skoll. The old Norse people believed that when a solar eclipse occurred this meant that the god of wolves had gotten closer the Sol which caused her lights to diminish. The wolf god won't be able to catch Sol until the time of Ragnarok.

Var

It is believed that the Norse goddesses were the one who kept track of oaths as well as the one who punished swearing infractions. In the past, in Norse society, a lot of trust was placed into a solemn vow that a person could only be as true as the word he spoke. Var had a dark figure who was often invited to oath ceremonies in order to make sure that the people who made the oaths adhered to their vows. If they did not her, she had the authority to punish the perpetrators.

Vor

Wisdom goddess was wife of Frigg. She was a skilled seeress, and she would inform Frigg what was to come in the near future. Her name translates to "awareness," and her abilities help people look into the future, and also provide clarity. Vor can be described as the god of honesty, and can help you get your life back in the right order. Vor is brutal and blunt and is well-known as a guru who can assist you tidy up your mess.

Yggdrasil

It is the tree that lives. appears as a goddess due to the nurturing qualities it has, but no one classifies it as either male or female in the depths Asgard in the Asgard where the gods dwell within the living tree, Yggdrasil. Always green, this magical Ash tree extends its branches across the worlds, and is an important focal point for Asatru.

The most prominent inhabitants of the tree include an the eagle, a serpent and an animal called a squirrel. The eagle wasn't identified, while the serpent was named Nidhogg while the squirrel was called Ratatosk. The serpent and the eagle were antagonists and the sly squirrel would fuel the hatred by sending message between two enemies.

The eagle might say something in a rude way about the snake and Ratatosk would rush to inform Nidhogg. The serpent would then slap the eagle, and that vicious circle could flee and run. Ratatosk loved gossip and adored to prolong the drama. In the branches of Yggdrasil there were four stags that gave beauty and harmony for the trees.

The very first source of Yggdrasil was called Urds well. The root went right into Asgard and was the place where gods would gather to decide what the day's agenda would be. It also was the place in which the gods, the 3 goddesses of destiny lived. They were known as the Norn and Norn, they made the decisions for every newborn born in the kingdom of Midgard. They were accountable for bringing waters from the well and irrigating the roots of

Yggdrasil to ensure that the tree remained in good health and healthy.

Another root from Yggdrasil was called Mimir's well. Mimir was the most wise person to ever live, as well as his well was an source of information. Odin was so determined to acquire that knowledge that it was necessary to sacrifice an eye to drink the water of its well, and that's why he's the god with one eye.

The Vanir killed Mimir after the war of gods. Odin felt so angry that he returned his head to him to bless it with magic herbs. It was strong that the head came back to life. Odin would talk to the head of Mimir to make difficult decisions.

A third celestial root in Yggdrasil was also known as the Well of Hvergelmir and brought us to the gruesome area known as Niflheim which was where Hel resided along with her deceased and her companions. Nidhogg came frequently and was known to drink the blood of the souls who were that were sent to live in the dark and vile world that Hel reigned.

Alongside the goddesses and gods There are some amazing creatures from Norse mythology. Here are a few of them:

Creatures originate from Norse Mythology

We are aware that gods and goddesses from Norse mythology were unpredictable and susceptible to human traits and thus more easily accessible. The mythology also is filled with magical creatures that both assist the gods, and also can be a danger to them. Certain creatures are companions of gods, and others are their children.

Audumbla

Audumbla is a mythical cow that fed the first giants on earth with her milk. She is among the first beings to have inhabited the planet and was the one responsible for licking the salt stone in order to reveal the final resting place of Buri who was the father of all gods. While she vanishes into the space between the ether and the universe after she created it but she is a key role in the evolution of the world.

Heidrun

Heidrun is a mythical goat, who is featured in tales that are part of both Poetic or Prose Edda. She is a mystical goat who eats the magical buds of the trees close to Valhalla and turns them into a mead which is so pure and clear the taste is like heaven. She is extremely careful to restrict her consumption of buds in order to continue to make mead to her warriors to sip on their horns for duration of time while they wait for Ragnarok and the final fight.

Huginn and Muggin

They may seem like they are from Sesame Street or the Harry Potter novel, but they were the eyes of Odin's ears. The mythical ravens would fly in the air and then return to the powerful god to whisper into his ears. Their names are a reference to thoughts and minds, and they are carrion bird species. they'd bring gifts to Odin in the battleground. Ravens signify that Odin is close or has accepted your present.

Tanngrisnir and Tanngnjostr

These are the magnificent goats that can pull a Chariot of Thor. The day begins with killing the two goats and eating their meat before returning them to life using his hammer. While Loki as well as Thor were on their way, they enjoyed a meal of caprine with an unlucky family. one of his sons was so full that he consumed the marrow of the bones. When Thor revived his goats one of them was suffering from an injury due to the absence of the marrow. Instead of scolding the boy, Thor made him his servant and he travelled with the god throughout the remainder of his life.

Jotunn

The common name for giants, Jotunn, is a prominent part of Norse mythology. They were usually found inside their very own world, named Jotunheimr However, they were frequently seen within Midgard and Asgard since the gods saw to them as lovers. The term "giant" isn't always an indication of their dimensions. While some were massive some were just similar to the size of the gods. The mythology of giants describes them as being some of the most stunning creatures that have ever been seen, or as ugly creatures that are difficult to see. Giants can be found at either one side of the attractive scale , or one side; there's not an acceptable middle, visually speaking.

Elves

They are small and cheerful in contemporary fantasy, but Norse mythology is a completely different story. Elves can be either dark or light, and work above and beneath the ground. They are described by the light-elves as being beautiful and with the same lightness like the sun. They only meet with humans when they are required to get rid of illnesses or are cursed to be sick. They prefer to be with Gods, and would prefer living among the stars.

The dark elves are different and their appearance is described as dark as pitch. They are cruel and brutal creatures, who are the official enemies of Asgardians. They are able to use tricks and deceit to get their way, and are the precursors to the elves in contemporary fantasy novels. They do not respect their fellow elves and have no regard for their fellow elves. They frequently engage in war with each other and other races.

The Fossegrim

He is an amazing water spirit who plays most beautiful music on his violin , while laying at the bottom of the sea, half-dressed. He'll draw males and females at the shore and assure them that they can learn how to play his violin. The first step is to sacrifice an animal in his name. If the goat is thin, he will teach them how to tune the violin. However, If it's big and delicious, he'll instruct them on how to play. The music they create will be so enchanting that it can make trees dance and they will be playing until their fingers start to bleed. The man is also known for luring girls and women into his property and then letting them drown so that they can join his swollen family.

Dwarves

The master craftsmen from Norse mythology were the dwarves. They were a squat-like race ugly creatures, who derived from the grubs, who consumed the corpse of Ymir. The writer Tolkein utilized the names of dwarves that were mentioned within the Poetic Edda for his dwarf characters, who were depicted as hardworking and intelligent. In Norse mythology the dwarves were evil and wicked, however their role is to be a part of the Gods and Goddesses made use of them in the creation of their weapons and jewels. They were a part of Svartalfheim in the north of Norway. Despite the modern definition of dwarves is a bit small and slender however, their height is not discussed as such in Norse stories. Actually, a portion of Norse mythology refers the dwarves as "holding the dome of the sky aloft," which is not a task that you would assign to someone person who is less than three feet tall.

Modern fairy tales also portray them as being more sinister as compared to their Norse counterparts due to the fact that they were underground and worked in forges. Christian beliefs depict the hell of Hell as an ablaze spot where Satan's furnaces keeps the dead in torture for the rest of eternity. It is believed that the concept of evil dwarves grew from this idea. When compared to the elves that reside above the earth, there appears to be an "devils and angels" concept that transcends the idea that was originally derived that came from Norse myths.

The Einherjar

Though they were fiercely dressed in their armor , and engaged in battle in the courtyards of Valhalla however, the Einherjar aren't a threat for mortals. They are the warriors who have been defeated chosen for joining Odin at his halls in preparation for their final fight of Ragnarok. Their name means "those who fight alone," however, they are also linked to the Germanic tribe that was famous for their fierceness and brutality during combat. They were the Roman expert Tacitus recorded their story in the first century AD. He wrote about them appearing out of the hills, covered with black paint, and with a savage shields of black to defend themselves. They attacked in the night and left destruction in their aftermath.

The description suggests an unimaginable army that would not be as effective in daylight hours, which is the reason why their name was changed to reflect the massive force comprised of Odins dead warriors that battle. Their bizarre and sinister appearance suggests they had no resemblance whatsoever to the living people. Einherjar are Einherjar were also described as warriors with fervor who were so committed to Odin that they would sacrifice their blood to gods in their honor. The picture of Odin dressed in his golden armor leading these combative warriors is a key aspect of the final moments of this world when they will be facing the big Wolf Fenrir in Ragnarok.

To prepare for their final fight In preparation for their final battle, the Einherjar would eat wild boar Saehrimnir every night, and wash the delicious pork down with mead made from the udders of an ethereal goat named Heidrun. Whatever number of warriors were in the grand halls of Valhalla the meat and mead were plentiful. Odin was a fierce warrior who drove his men throughout the day, but they were rewarded with drinks and food provided by the Valkyrie the of Odin's war maidens. The Valkyrie were more than servers in Valhalla. They were the shield bearers of Odin who watched the battlegrounds and selected those brave warriors enough to be able to join Odin as well as his armies of Einherjar.

Chapter 4: The Poetic Edda

Much of what we know concerning Norse gods, religions and myths is derived out of the Poetic as well as the Prose Edda books. They are the most important source of information on the Norse traditions which were written and published by Snorri Sturluson during the 13th century.

The translations available are mostly German and English however they differ due to the fact that they are both written in the Old Norse language is intricate and is difficult to define fully. The significance of these poems is incalculable and they have shaped the basis of our beliefs about how Norse people lived and fought for, as well as believed in Gods and Goddesses. These poems offer vivid accounts of heroic actions, hilarious characters, and stunning images, which makes them both fascinating and instructive.

The uncertainty surrounding the translations make that Poetic Edda even more significant. Many experts believe that it is an improbable publication that contains separate poems that are not in a particular order, whereas others consider it to be an exhaustive description of Norse beliefs. For those who are new to the subject the poetry edda offers the manuscript of poetry and stories which introduces you to the principal characters in Norse mythology.

Despite the numerous debates and arguments about the prose and origins to the texts, stories of the Poetic Edda are entertaining and thrilling. The poems are split into mythological and heroic lay. Another publication called Codex Regius includes stories that certain experts put within the Poetic Edda index and others do not. Let the experts and historians fight to settle their disputes and battles while we take a look at some of the stories in the Edda to learn more about who our villains are and what they stand for.

The Voluspa is also known by the name of Prophecy of the Seeress, that tells how the world came into existence. The text is written in the form of a volva, or a Norse seeress tells the story to Odin who is the father of gods. She informs him about his existence as Ymir and his world, which was only filled with The Aesir following his demise. The poem is among the most popular poems in Norse mythology.

Havami is a small volume of poetry that offers advice on how to live a healthy and moral life. It is also referred to by the Sayings of Har.

The Ballad of Vafthrudnir is a poem that recounts an exchange with Odin, Frigg, and the gigantic Vafthrudnir about the universe.

The Ballad of Grimnir is another poem that focuses on Odin and offers wisdom from Odin's Allfather.

Loki's fight is the 7th poem in the Edda and is about Loki's moral deficiency in his ultimate binding. Even though mythology tells us that Loki was penalized for his role in the demise of Baldur but this poem does not clarify that. It depicts Loki at his most vile and focuses on the hatred that other gods held for Loki. Interactions among Loki and his old friend Odin are particularly tense.

The Lay of Volund

The Ballad of Alvis is the story of a dwarf called Alvis trying to get the bride of Thor. Thor is unable to accept and assigns the dwarf the task of having to answer all of his questions in order to be married to his child. Thor will then ask the dwarf an endless set of questions, which he answers with accuracy. But, when the sun rises above horizon the dwarf gets struck by its rays and changes to stone. Thor admits later that it was his scheme and he thwarted Alvis to prevent him from getting married to his daughter.

Baldur's Dream tells the story about the god Baldur prediction of his own demise that led to his mother Freya shifting heaven and earth to prevent the event from occurring. Loki plays a major role in the demise of Baldur which results in his fate changing for ever. The poem is some of the more enduring stories about the goddesses and gods as well as the way they interacted. Their shortcomings and traits are evident for everyone to see. It is a dramatic tale with a an unsettling ending.

The Song of Rig is a poem that describes the ways in which Rig created the three human classes. The poem is set in the home of his great-grandfather Ai as well as his spouse Edda. Rig was given a poor dinner and a very poor shelter during the night. Nine months after his departure, Edda gave birth to an infant son, named

Prael who was small and ugly. He was the father of the serfs.

The following night Rig spent the night with a crafter named Afi as well as his partner, Amma. He was fed food that was modest, and his accommodation was adequate. Nine months after, Amma gave birth to the son Karl who was a handsome boy with a bright smile and a kind nature who later became his father to the craftsmen and farmers.

Rig had a wonderful evening with the couple called Faoir and Mooir in their luxurious home. He was treated to a lavish dinner and the finest wine he'd ever tasted. Nine months after, Mooir gave birth to an adorable blue-eyed and blonde-haired son. The family gave him the name Jarl. The boy was very adept in the field and handled horses. Rig returned home after a while and returned to his son, urging him to seek out lordship. Jarl later fathered the race of Lords and Jarls who controlled over the Norse world.

The Ballad of Svipdag

The Spell of Groa is the name given to The necromancer Groa which returned back to Earth after her demise. She returned to assist her son defeat his treacherous stepmother. The poem is connecting necromancy to Asatru and gods.

The Ballad of Fjoisvid

Odins Raven Chant The tale of Odin and an assortment of gods and goddesses who visit Midgard. Midgard to save an unknown human female who has the ability to predict what the future holds for the planet. They inquire of her what she knows about the present, beginning as well as future universe as well as heaven and Hel. She doesn't respond with words and weeps. They return with the gods to

Asgard The poem ends with Heimdall raising his horn towards the sky.

Heroic Poems and Lays of the Poetic Edda

The death of Sinfjotl is the tale that tells of the son of Sgmindr's loss at the hands that of his stepmother. She gives him two ale horns which are poisonous to him therefore, he left the horns. The third horn arrived and his father assured him that it was safe. He drank it, and passed away quickly.

The Ballad of Regin

The Ballad of Fafnir is the tale of the guardian dragon Fafnir and the way Sigurd consumed his heart to discover the birds.

Fragment of a Sigurd Lay

The First Lay of Gudrun is an epic poem that tells an account of deep grief loss, death, and grief. Gudrun recounts the story while sitting beside her husband who has passed away as she is visited by family members to mourn her loss. The family members all recount stories of loss and death and discuss the burial of their loved ones with their hands. The poem has been hailed for being among the most powerful of the Eddas.

The Short Lay of Sigurd

The Hel Ride of Brunhilde is an epic tale that involves Sigurd as well as Brunhilde and is considered to be one some of the greatest poems of the collection. It's a sweet love story that concludes with the couple being duped into separating. Brunhilde concludes the poem by saying that women and men live in this world to be hurt, but she and her lover will discover a way to be together in the next world.

The Slaying of the Nuflings is the poem that relates the aftermath of Brunhilde's death. It's a bloody tale of violence and serpents , involving treachery and betrayal. The runes communicate a message to the magic ring known as Andvarnaut which could be used to locate silver and gold.

The second Lay of Gudrun is a poem that focuses on the grief of Gudrun after the loss of a number of warriors in an enthralling battle. She tells King Atli her story of the loss of Sigurd and her love lost. Her mother then entices her to get married to an Hun warrior and she accepts the offer even though she doesn't like the man. Her heart breaks, and the poem closes with speculation about whether her demise is thought of as an act of sacrifice.

The Third Lay of Gudrun is an review of her life and the accusation she received of lying to someone who wasn't her husband. She denies her innocence and requests the sacred kettle to go through the arduous task of boiling water in order to demonstrate her faith. She receives justice and is found innocent.

The Lament of Oddrun

The Lay of Atli is the story of an ancestor to Atilla The Hun and is centered around his request of joining forces with leaders. It is a story about warriors' courage, the way they smile even under pressure, and concludes with a fiery battle in the halls at Gudrun.

The interpretations of these historic poems have changed over the years. The intricate original texts have led to different interpretations and also mean that they do not have an established English analog. The oldest translation dates from the 17th century, whereas the most current version is only two years older. The Voluspa poem is available in at least twelve translations that are diverse, but all of them remain true to the core of the text.

The characters in poetry have become the topic of debate Some scholars claim they are real-life characters and others claiming these are fictional. The date of to the Eddas is also controversial since some art forms are considered to be as old as the ninth century however, some poems may be of the 12th or 13th century. Since the tales have been passed down from generation to generation through the word of mouth They could have components as old as that of Roman Iron Age, which was in existence from 1AD up to 400AD.

Does this mean that the stories are any less interesting? Actually, the atmosphere of mystery surrounding these stories only makes them more fascinating. Who created the elements? And when? We'll probably never get an answer definitively however, it doesn't matter. They've given us a vivid and dramatic background upon which the entire belief system was built.

The Prose Edda is more concerned with the notions of Norse lifestyle and beliefs. It states that the universe is divided into 3 distinct parts The SW was called Africa The West, towards the north was Europe and the rest of the region was Asia. The center of the globe was the city of Troy in the region of Troy, where the soil was fertile and Troy was the biggest settlement ever discovered by man. The gods mentioned by the Prose Edda differ from the gods of the Poetic Edda but have similar traits and characteristics.

It's an act of gods, not the tales of poetic poetry found inside The Poetic Edda but is as crucial as the other.

Chapter 5: The Noble Virtues of Asatru

While it is called an faith, Asatru is based on general guidelines, not an established doctrine. At first there was no term for the religion, but it was a religion that Nordic people were following from prehistoric times. The people who adhered to it were part of a larger community who adhered to a specific ethical code and lived the right way. Old Norse people believed in living in a communal way and living their lives in accordance with the guidelines given by their gods and goddesses.

The term Asatru is derived of the Scandinavian language spoken in people of the Old Norse and means Asa as a symbol of "of the Gods" and Tru - which is the idea of faith and loyalty. The adherents of Asatru are more of an extended family rather than a religious group. They are collectively referred to as the Asafolk that translates to "kinfolk," and they consider that all followers are part of their family as well as their kin. Although there is no official written creed that they must adhere to They think that being a part of the family automatically connects them to the other followers. Morals and ethics they adhere to are what makes their bonds indestructible.

Their fundamental beliefs are based on the human action and the impact they have on people as well as their surroundings. There are benefits for good actions, and punishments for bad behaviour when looking at other religions. Morality and sin isn't present in Asatru There aren't punishments or rewards in an uncertain future. Asatru is focused on the present moment and how it's lived. This way the followers of Asatru are in control of their destiny and are able to decide their destiny in their own hands.

The benefits of this manner of living are evident in the present and people think that every positive experience they have by the present moment will carry over into their future lives. It is not a "original sin," and no action they take will be a mark on their souls. Asatru is a non-religion of guilt that holds that all of us are accountable for our own ethical choices and that any wrong act has the consequences. They do not believe in atonement or penance and prefer the common sense approach to life. If you're a good person and live your life according to your values and values, you'll be rewarded by your own choices. It isn't necessary to follow "commandments" or strict guidelines and aren't a sheep waiting for a shepherd to teach them how to live. They have the freedom to make decisions, think and act in a manner that reflects their beliefs about certain qualities.

The Poetic Edda, the Havamal book provides information on how people of the Old Norse people practiced Asatru. It is a straightforward text that provides advice on ethics, morals, as well as simple ways to become an improved person. The information and advice included in this book has been employed to form a basic outline for modern organizations that will adhere to the ways of Asatru. They are also known by The Nine Noble Virtues, although certain followers employ different names and phrases to describe the virtues and the integrity.

They aren't a set of laws or commands and aren't restricted to Asatru followers. These are the principles that we all should follow and constitute a fundamental quality of a healthy life.

The Nine Noble Virtues of Asatru (And How to Achieve Them)

1. Courage

In earlier times, courage typically meant courage on the battlefield , and was believed to be a virtue for warriors. It is a good thing that we're not required to engage in these types of battles in our contemporary times. Courage is a different concept for us. For us, fighting is still important, however, we must all embrace more of a broader sense of courage. Being a devoted adherent of Asatru is not easy, because there are many who will not agree with your views and beliefs. Make sure you are able to stand up and affirm your beliefs despite the threat of reprisals might be present.

How to Show Courage Every Day

Dream Bigger

Are you feeling secluded by the world or people who surround you? Are you involved in a relationship that works for you, but has come to an end? Take inspiration from your dreams and believe that they're achievable. Take on the dream job you've always wanted, plan that trip that will last a lifetime, and strive for the stars. Don't let fear stop you from achieving your goals. The biggest risk in your life be your goals aren't big enough and you'll not be able to succeed, not that they're too big which is why you can't!

Be Who You Are

The demand to be conformist has never been more intense but the opportunity to create your own identity is now more readily available. What is your identity? Do you pretend as someone different to please others? It might sound like a way to live a selfless living, but it is basically deceiving yourself as well as to others. Be real and accept your character because if you conform to the norm to the norm, you only provide. If you're genuine, you give it all you have.

Speak Up

Make sure you are the person who keeps their head over the parapet and voice your worries. Be respectful of others and their opinions, however be prepared to engage in uncomfortable conversations. Sometimes, it's best to have difficult conversations in order to ensure that any unsolved requirements aren't left unanswered. Talking up can help you build your self-worth and helps you express what you consider to be crucial.

Say No

Yes is a common option for some people and can be perceived as a kind and thoughtful gesture. But, having the courage to say no is a sign that you're being honest with yourself and allowing the positive things that happen in your life.

Set boundaries and provide clear indications of what you're a firm believer in, what you're willing to accept and what you won't.

Let Go

Asatru is all about having faith in your own actions and the way you conduct your life. But every person has baggage and gets dependent on external influences. Don't try to manage what's outside your reach and focus on the things you can control. Do not waste time and energy trying to figure out what others are thinking and doing So, find the courage to release and go forward.

2. Truth

An easy to define virtue, honesty should be a symbol of respect for yourself. Asatru adherents believe that a crime can be made more difficult when one lies to cover up their actions. How can you stay clear of these kinds of deceit? Don't do anything people shouldn't care about. Truth is the only universal ingredient that connects us all.

The act of lying is exhausting. it is important to remember what you've told the truth as well as the other strands of your web of lies.

How to be More Truthful Every Day

Stop the White Lies

The word "white lie" conveys the idea that it's acceptable to lie even if the topic isn't crucial. This isn't a good method of living. It is still lying. So, try to tell the truth even in the event that it hurts. Falsehood is another untrue term. It's lying to cover up your appearance. If you've previously told someone an untruth so that they feel good, you should consider the truth in your talk to them.

Be truthful about social situations.

If you decide to cancel plans or arrive late to work, do you admit to the truth about the reason? Take a different approach in the event that you've made up a reason to not meeting with your friends or family or blamed your tardiness due to traffic instead of admitting that you got up early. You must be honest and offer your reasons in a clear and honest manner for your behavior.

Be Honest in Your Relationships

Be truthful without being harsh. Make sure you use positive words and maintain your emotions under control in conversations that are honest. If, for instance, you're consistently late for a acquaintance, do not start conflict, but instead have an open discussion. You can be able to say "I altered my schedule to get here on time, but you are twenty minutes late. I could have spent that time working. Please consider my time when we make arrangements to meet."

If you're angry enough to engage in a calm conversation and you are not sure how to proceed, tell the truth. "I am too upset to talk right now; we should speak later when I have calmed down so we can address our issues."

Find out what you can do to be sincere and kind while employing positive language and by being helpful. If you see someone struggling at work You can ask whether they require assistance and then point out areas that require improvement. Don't be a nuisance to people's feelings and don't put them in shame in front of other people.

3. Honor

The underlying principle of the Asatru argument is honor. Without it, one is useless. What exactly is honor? Simply put, there's an expression that says "Reputation is what others say about you; honor is what you know to be true about yourself." It's an amalgamation of all other virtues, and is the moral compass you need to always adhere to. It's not just about your own self-respect. It's equally about how you treat others. Honoring yourself and respecting the honor of others should be an everyday thing you do.

How to Show Honor Every Day

Pay Compliments When They Are Appropriate

Giving a compliment isn't easily to the majority of people. The reactions they get can be mixed and awkward. But that shouldn't stop you from being gracious when someone is doing something worthy of being praised or honoured.

Keep Good Company

It is a group Your company's image ought to reflect the same. Being around individuals who motivate you as well as act as models can ensure that you maintain your integrity and become part of a truly respected group.

Honor Your Word

If you make a promise to do something, make sure you don't violate that promise. You've made a commitment that is more valuable than any other form of currency. Keep in mind that you're trustworthy when you say something and if you violate your word, you violate the trust of those who trust you. Make yourself the person who can be trusted to stick to their commitment to their.

Cheer Someone On

The act of encouraging others should come naturally. If we all took on the role of being a source of encouragement for other people then the world would be an even more prosperous place. Imagine a society that is tolerant of accomplishments rather than one that attempts to make people feel down. If you are taking on new challenges, it is beneficial to have someone else with you to help Be that person who goes the extra mile to inspire others. If they accomplish their goals, ensure that you thank them for their efforts honestly. Honor is when you're not in a position to be jealous or angry about other people's achievements.

Engage

What do you feel like when you are in conversation with you but they have some other thing on their mind? Feeling disregarded, angry and probably ignored. It's not acceptable to be less than per cent active when someone is talking with you. So be attentive. When you need to, ask questions and pay attention to what they say. You'd expect this level of respect from other people therefore, make sure to provide it without hesitation.

Communicate

Send a brief email or text message to inquire about someone's status. are doing. There is no other reason for it, simply asking how they're doing is a sign that you think of them and appreciate their position on the planet. Honor doesn't mean grand gestures. It's about understanding that each and every human is a unique individual with qualities that deserve to be acknowledged and celebrated.

Forgive

A grudge can be unhealthy. It can be a drain on your soul and can cause you to be angry So forgiveness isn't only a way to help other people feel better. It also assists you in achieving an improved mental balance. Everyone is not perfect, and mistakes do happen, even if you've suffered harm due to the actions of someone else are to blame, you have the power to be the stronger man and forgive them.

4. Fidelity

Sometimes referred to in the term loyalty quality connects Asatru adherents to their gods and goddesses as well as their kin. The fidelity you show to your beliefs and your circle of friends is a great method of showing your respect and love for them. Remain faithful to those around you by these methods. In Norse times, keeping oaths essential, and some of bloodiest battles were lost over broken swearing.

How to Show Fidelity Every Day

Give Space When Requested

Sometimes, we require time to ourselves even when we're in a romantic relationship. Giving your partner an area to themselves is a mark of love and respect. You believe in them being loyal to you, just as you're loyal to them.

Be Your Partner's Defender

As a team, ensure that your team members are there for you when they have a conflicts. That doesn't mean you have to help them in instances where they're not right; that's encouraging, but supporting them when they're in need is an indication of loyalty. You trust them, and you're committed for their goals.

Stop others from gossiping about the people you love

If you see a group of people who are discussing someone in the family or a friend be sure to intervene and tell that they should be more respectable and stop talking about them. You might not be the most famous person in the group, but you'll have the highest loyalty. Selling your fidelity to get noticed is a part of the Asatru method.

5. Discipline

There are various types of discipline, however it is self-discipline when applied to Asatru convictions. It requires an internal moral compass that lets you be aware of when tempting morally oriented distractions affect you. The two go together to ensure that you remain loyal to Asatru's beliefs as well as the religion that is the faith of Norse gods. Asatru adherents tend to stay away from their faith and try other religions. They recognize the right of others to explore other religions but prefer to stick to their beliefs.

How to Show Discipline Every Day

Plan a Routine

Find inspiration from the elite athletes and develop an outline to follow. They know when it is time to exercise, rest, and break for meals and enjoy some time off. They have a routine that they follow which makes it automatic and you can follow the same. You wake up at the same time and fall asleep at a specific time to ensure that you are getting enough sleep. Set your meal times at specific hours and prepare your menu in the months ahead. The shopping process should always include a checklist, which will help to budget and stay organized.

Commit to the End

Have you ever attended an academic course and then dropped out within a few minutes of classes? This is an obvious sign of an inability to keep a consistent schedule. If you are considering a new endeavor or commitment be sure to consider the effort and time it will take. Prepare yourself for a long-term commitment even when encounter difficulties. Don't be a quitter. Enjoy the process of working hard and conquering the obstacles. Self-improvement can be a great stimulant. The more you work it, the greater the amount. Discipline is the source of power and it allows you the ability to go beyond the normal boundaries and discover your talents and abilities.

Build a No Matter What Mindset

The change in your mindset can help you continue to work until the end of each project you take on. The pressure you place on yourself will force you past the negativity and give you the determination to finish the task. Whatever you do you're doing, you'll be there, and the satisfaction you experience will be unforgettable.

6. Hospitality

The past was a time when people were left stranded and many people recognized the necessity of turning their homes safe refuges for those who traveled. The foundation of our civilization has to do with the way it makes up the social fabric of society. We are now more cautious and consider travelers and strangers as threats. Sometimes, we have valid reasons to justify this way of thinking, however we're a bit more cautious at sometimes.

Should we be welcoming every stranger to our home? Absolutely not, that is a mistake and could pose a risk to our homes, but what happens if you find out that the person you're inviting has a connection to Asatru community? Be sure to take safety precautions, but also let your home and mind to people from other cultures and ensure that they feel welcomed. The practice dates back to the Old Norse when the gods of Asatru wandered around the world of Midgard which is the place that we live in as a disguised entity. Asatru taught his followers to open their doors to strangers because you can never know who they are and it is possible to serve refreshments to someone belonging to the Aesir or the Vanir.

How to Practice Hospitality Every Day

If you're not willing to let your home be open consider these alternate ways to show your hospitality to strangers:

Share Food

In the event that you make a cake, make double the recipe, then donate the items that you don't require. Banana bread or cookies might be a small snack for your family, but they could be a blessing to someone. Wrap your gift in white paper, and deliver them by hand. Don't limit gifts to occasions of celebration; they should be freely given and with affection.

If you know someone who just had a child, offer her to a special cup of coffee or plate of muffins to kick off your day. Motherhood can be stressful, and all new moms feel the stress. Give her something special only for her. People frequently forget mom once their baby arrives and all gifts are all geared towards the baby.

Offer Help

What can you do to help an individual you're acquainted with? Babysitting? Do you want to invite their children along to your own family gathering? What you do can constitute an act of kindness and kindness. Offering someone a few unsupervised hours can be as beneficial as gifting them a relaxing day.

Talk to Someone Who Is Bereaved

If someone dies the family members who are left behind may feel so isolated that they may feel as if they're breaking. If you write a letter or condolence card including your phone number or email address and inform that you're there to talk with them whenever they're in need of one. You can fill in a gap for their needs and be there whenever they're in need of a conversation.

7. Industriousness

You've never seen an unmotivated Viking and the beliefs of Asatru are based on a disciplined approach to all aspects of life. Do your best to meet your goals, then put that effort into other things. Be aware that every day may be the last day of your life and make the most of the time you have left on this earth to show the world that you do not take your life lightly.

Create a habit of hard work like these:

* Reduce your To-Do List to size What are the number of things that you need to do on the list? Are they all of them relevant or do you think you could improve your performance by reducing the amount and redirecting your attention to the most crucial things?

* Rest: Those who are productive recognize the benefits of taking breaks on a regular basis. If your body or your brain is hurting, it is sending the message that it is time to take a break. Be attentive and obey.

* Stop multitasking: There is a common belief that multitaskers can be more efficient, but this isn't actually the case. They are skilled at multitasking and are more likely to abandon them in the

middle. If you shift the subject matter of your mind it reduces your brain's ability to be imaginative and efficient. Focus on one task at a given time and complete the job done quickly, but efficiently.

* Disconnect from distractions What are the times you've been in the tunnel of social media distraction only to discover that it's been twenty minutes but you've not done anything? Think about having two devices, one for work and a social , which means that the temptation to check your social networks is diminished.

8. Self-Reliance

This is another method to ensure you don't rely on anyone else to get the job accomplished. Nowadays, jobs are being handed over to an absurd extent. We aren't capable of doing things on our own. In Asatru the gods honored those that stood up on feet. They identify with those who aren't content with asking for handouts , but instead use their abilities and know-how to stay alive. There are many methods to be more self-sufficient and self-sufficient, such as the ones that follow:

Learn a useful skill such as plumbing, carpentry and electrical basics mean you can DIY without the need to hire contractors.

• Begin composting in order to feed your garden, reducing consumption and making your soil healthier.

* Avoid using disposable items such as paper plates and plastic bottles.

* Plant fruit trees and vegetable plants in your garden to provide for yourself.

Create your own organic cleaning products to keep your clean and never be without cleaning supplies ever again.

* Cook From Scratchfrom scratch: Do not rely on the commercial food outlets and re-discover the pleasure of cooking from scratch.

* Learn to fix items, which will can reduce the amount of the amount of waste and also save money.

9. Perseverance

The last benefit of Asatru is the most important in the religious teachings. It is a demonstration of what a committed group can accomplish when they collaborate to reach the finish line. Kinship is all about standing into the spotlight when you are feeling confident and lifting the burden off people who are feeling overwhelmed.

How to Develop Perseverance and Persistence

Use Visualization

Create a vision board that will aid you in focusing upon your objectives. Visual aids in cultivating the growth mindset and provides the fuel for your thoughts. If you can visualize your goals as a matter of fact, they will be more pertinent.

Find a Successful Role Model

There is always something to learn from other people, and finding positive role models can aid you in your pursuit instead of losing hope. Take a look at the number of publishers who have turned J.K. Rowling away before she achieved success. What was the number of record companies that have scoffed at the Beatles and sent them back down the route? It's not easy to achieve success Don't let failures hinder your progress.

Be a Lifelong Learner

If you are willing to learn by embracing learning, you are setting yourself up to be successful. A curious mind will go to any lengths to seek answers and expand your possibilities. Explore new things each day, and you will become a sponge for soaking all the knowledge that you are seeking.

Chapter 6: The Tools of the Asatru and Basic Rituals

Although the rituals, rites and connection to gods do not rely on tools or magic objects, the reverence of gods, divinities, and the connection to the past generations could be enhanced by specific objects. They boost the energy level and set out intentions using tools was the first thing that differentiated us from other species of mammals. Utilizing tools made humans more efficient and grow. In the art form of Norse paganism and Asatru are not distinct. Tools help us concentrate on the task at being done, and every tool has a function to perform.

These tools are not required, and like any other aspect of religion, you can choose which you choose to use and what you don't. They are however powerful tools to let go of the realm of Midgard and reconnect to your spiritual realm when you use them. They can be an intermediary between the world of humankind as well as the realm of gods. You can enter the realm of nine realms and express your intentions using your tools. They are able to speak with a voice that is stronger over yours. They can be a powerful force for your actions and declare your intentions.

The tools were given to us by the legends from the Asatru. They've not changed over the years and provide symbolic objects that link us directly to the realm from and the Norse gods. They'll instantly understand the tools you employ that haven't changed in decades. Imagine trying to get in touch with that spirit in your great grandfather and you utilized phones or computers to transmit your message. It could confuse you as well, making your messages difficult to comprehend.

We utilize ancient tools and equipment to communicate with the gods and forms an experience that is shared with this connection in our minds. Use the tools that inspire you to help you in your work, and keep them from other people. They should be fuelled solely by your own energy except to perform rituals that are shared, and they are energized by the other participants. Avoid using them in the household for routine tasks since they'll be lost in their sacredness.

Below is a listing of tools and products that are available on the internet or at specialist stores. Select the ones that you have a strong affinity for and like; this type of shopping can be good for your soul:

Bowl Bowl: Hlautbolli from Asatru is the bowl used in ceremonies that was used to sprinkle liquids on the level of a Blot or Simbel. Bowls were used in order to capture the sacrifice's blood mentioned in the ancient texts and was a crucial element in the ceremony. Blood was considered sacred and carried the energy of an offering to nine gods' realms. Offering bowls decorated with runes and different Viking symbols are sold at less than $40. They are a sacred instrument that is practical as well as mysterious.

Drinking Horn: Also known as the Drekkjar during Norse time, it was the horn that soldiers and wives would consume mead or ale while eating. The mead would be served in the bowl and then distributed among others at the gathering in the blot. There is no expectation that you would kill a stag or der, and then hollow it out for drinking from, therefore a variety of options are readily available on the internet. In accordance with the size and the material the horn is made of, you can purchase glass, wooden or even plastic drinking horns that cost between $20 and $100.

Wand: Also known as the Stav Wand, it was an object of wood that was utilized to channel energies during rituals. It's a simple piece of your preferred ash, cedar or oak tree is all you need as well, or you can buy more expensive.

Incense Burners: Also known as Recels and you can make use of normal burners or purchase items that are themed to Norse. A few Gothi are known to use the burners to produce the perfect cleansing smoke, bathing the guests with the scent. You can make this at home with the use of a small flame and fan. Burn your preferred incense and let the smoke circulate to spread over you and clean the area.

Altar The most crucial component of your toolbox the altar was referred to as the Stalli when indoors, and the Harrow for outdoor use. Certain practitioners use both, based on the magic they prefer. Rituals and spells that are performed under the glow of the moon and sun are more powerful than spells performed inside. You can build your own altar using natural materials or purchase an already-built altar. There are a variety of altars available as well as portable altars that allow you to practice Asatru regardless of where you are in the moment. The most basic altar tables can be purchased for less than $20. they can be embellished with altar cloths that make them more useful and less prone to being damaged.

The Moot Horn A carved horn that has an opening in the middle which summons the loved one to a gathering or celebration. You can find them in music stores, or even mystical pagan supplies shops. If you think a horn can sound too extreme, you could use other instruments that sound to summon your clans like tambourines, singing bowls, or even tambourines. Noise and music are an integral part of celebrating life, and there's no bad choices.

Oath Ring The Oath Ring that the gods were attracted to oaths, and many of the bloodiest battles were fought when swearing was broken. Oath rings were an integral part of the procedure, and was used to strengthen relationships and to make acquaintances into a kindred. Make use of the positive energy from an oath ring as a way to swear your loyalty to another and you'll feel the strength of the relationship. Rings that depict Odin, Thor, or Skadi are particularly meaningful.

Runes and a Casting Board

If you are planning to use runes to divinate then you must select a set that is suitable for your requirements. These Elder

Futhark runes are the most well-known runes available that are available and are accessible for every budget. They are comprised of 24 symbols, and have defined meanings. As with any Asatru or Norse practice, one are able to decide to interpret the meanings based on your own beliefs.

How to Read the Runes

These are the most commonly used runes that are part of the Elder Futhark set, and below is the general topic for each. Certain meanings are derived from the texts of the past, and some have been altered to modern interpretations.

* Fehu domestic financial matters, finance and plenty

*Uruz: Aurochs strength, force, as well as breaking the barriers

*Thursaz Thor with his hammer The sound of the heavens and his hammer, the voice of the heavens and

"* Ansuz Odin is the voice of God and joint words of the universe

* Raido: The passage of time, physical and spiritual travel, as well as the wheel

* Kenaz Spirit and Fire and passion for the inside, and the power of force

"Globo": relationships marriage joy, and happiness

* Wunjo working together with your family to succeed as well as personal happiness and career heights

* Hagalaz Extreme weather, transformation change, and changes in conditions

* Naudiz: Recognize your personal requirements above all others, and self-fulfillment

* Isa Refresh to regroup, recharge and refresh

"Jera," a.k.a Jera, reaping the rewards from your work Physical rewards

* Elwaz: Strength, knowledge The tree of Life

* Pertho: Don't be afraid to take a chance and take risks and play the dice

* Algiz The Horn of Plenty breaking down barriers and resolving problems

* Sowilo: fire as well as solar power, moment of opportunity

* Tiwaz: The Rune of Tyr Legal issues, and the resolution of injustices

* Berkano She is the mother's protection and force of motherhood

"Ehwaz," Equine power, strong partnerships, and showing confidence in your kin

* Mannaz Join the group organization and speak out on your humanitarian concerns

* Laguz is a Flowing Energy as well as the ocean, and the natural source of water

*Ingwaz: Sexuality love, passion and fertility

* Othala: Passing on ancestral treasures family, home, and Balance

* Dagaz: Look for new opportunities and greet the new time

Similar to the way you find one or two jokers in a deck There may be a blank rune often referred to as"wyrd. "wyrd" that can mean fate or be used to give the meaning. Runes can help you understand what the issues you face and what solutions might are within the depths of your.

Casting is an additional option that is personal to each individual. Certain Norse seers would make use of pre-coated boards that have distinct sections to emphasize the meaning, while others utilized clean white cloths. Some seers would throw their beads into the sea or on the earth , if their goals were of nature.

Simple Casting Methods

The most convenient method of using the runes is to take the basic one from the bag. Rune bags are great to store your items however they also offer you the chance to select one completely randomly. Put your hands in the bags until you get the feeling of a specific rune. You can then take it out, and determine the meaning. For example drawing the Jera rune could mean that you'll be granted an increase in your job or a pay raise. It could also mean that you sell something that you've worked on for a while and get financially recognized.

Cast 3 Runes

This method can give you a better understanding of the rune as well as the procedure is exactly the same as a single rune casting method, however, instead of pulling three. When you have them in your palm put them on an object or table. Ask a question or allow the symbols to speak. If the runes fall face upwards, this is positive, but it could be a signal of caution or setback should they fall face down. Face-up runes could indicate that they are signalling a pressing issue while downward-facing runes aren't as crucial.

It is possible to include running direction into the therunes when they drop. The compass points have particular energies and deities. The Viking compass is made up of eight points. It was significant for them since it was a way to make journeys home more secure. Make an Viking compasses with eight points, and then use the eight gods to embellish it. Odin, Thor, Freya, Loki, Freyr, Frigg, Balder, and Tyr are all able to bring their unique magical qualities to your reading according to the way that the runes appear.

For instance for instance, if Othala is located in northern direction, this may indicate the stability of your finances and family issues or family matters. Prothro looking east could indicate that you should be risky with your money. Prepare yourself to think outside of the norm and observe what transpires.

The next next step would be to expand the amount of runes you can cast, and to gain greater meanings with each casting. Be patient and establish an association with your set since they must be able to comprehend you as you must be able to comprehend them. Keep your focus and energy pure. Do not let others handle them . Keep them in your bag in an area of sacred in which they are able to recharge.

If they get dirty, use gentle cleansing methods such as Dawn soap, warm water and soap. Dry them off and clean them with a gentle method. The care you give to your runes shows the respect you have for and belief in the Norse methods. It demonstrates your intentions and your faith in gods and the answers they offer.

The Casting Boards

The casting boards is a different option to boost your reding. It is decorated with sections which indicate specific areas of your life or specific Norse gods. There are a variety of designs available and they're decorative and a valuable part of your rune set. You can purchase your runes from pagan supply stores or pick up suggestions on Pinterest and Etsy to create your own.

Make Your Board Original and Personal

Select the material you wish to use. Slate, wood or any other natural materials are ideal for making boards, however you can begin your board using cardboard if you're not sure of the style you want to create. Make sure you practice the design until you are happy with it before transferring the design onto your desired surface.

Here are some suggestions to consider:

The Quarterly Board

What to Include:

Make your own board by dividing it into sections that are labeled

* The zone of reception

* The field of giving

* The decision-making area

* The question area

These sections may then be divided into different areas, and labeled

* Manifestation

* Causation

* Present

* Future

The runes on this board are able to be easily recognized and also dateable. They will be more meaningful and meaning once they are cast and it will allow you to clarify your concerns and questions more specific.

The Deities Board

Select your gods of choice and design a part of the board that is dedicated to them. Make use of their images, their preferences and animals to make an unique space to place your runes.

The Solar Board

Divide the board into seven sections, and select one planet that represents all seven sections. Make use of color and symbols to invoke the power of the sky and provide a source of casting to cast your own runes.

Practical Board

The board can be divided into eight parts, and mark them with the most important areas of your interest.

"Money: This area will be your financial situation that should reflect your financial situation. It is best decorated using coins or dollar bills. Your goal should be clear and easy to understand.

* Friends: Use images of your friends , or an abstract symbol such as handshakes to

symbolize friends in the present and future.

* Heart: The symbol of love is a great symbol of love. It could be an emotional bonding or affection for your family and friends. The heart is a lover different ways and it embodies that fact.

* Home: The space that you feel secure and secure. The word "home" can be used to describe a variety of shapes and forms but is symbolized by a simple rectangle that has a roof, windows and doors. Even if you reside within an apartment, or a different type of dwelling it is a symbol that is inclusive.

* Work: The way you earn money is among the most crucial areas that you will have to consider in the course of. The appearance of a computer or other tool can give the area a personal touch to your profession.

*Travel: This is the space for your travels and explorations. Make use of a plane or suitcase to symbolize travel. See what runes are bringing to your next travels.

Self Your needs, yourself and your goals are all areas that often require attention. Utilize a picture self-portrait or the mirror symbol to signify self-identification as well as your individual needs.

* Families: The term can mean different things to different people. the definition of what you consider to be family will differ based on your personal. What is your family? Show them in this space by using pictures or a generic picture of figures who have their arms wrapped around one another.

Elemental Board

The four elements are able to create four distinct zones on the boards. Air, fire, water and Earth are four elements which define our universe and are the most important to the board You can put circles to represent your inner mental state. Make beautiful images that symbolize the elements and incorporate gods and goddesses to enhance their significance.

Your board could be an evidence of your intentions as well as a treasured piece of your toolkit. It is possible to have multiple sets of runes as well as boards to make use of when you face particular issues.

Asatru Rituals

The Blot

In the ancient language of Norse the word"blot" is a reference to sacrifice. However, the word isn't used the same manner in the modern Asatru but has altered to refer to the offering of something ordinary changing to something sacred. If you are offering items to gods, ensure that you mention their names and include your request in the beginning before you make your offering. Give a reason why the gift you're giving is important and why it matters to you.

Stop the blot by using an expression such as "Du et Des," which is a reference to a present for you, or utilize English for making your intention more powerful. Pick a phrase that matches your expectations regarding the outcome however, it is a formal end.

Feasting

It's exactly what it is. The preparation of a large meal and sharing a joyous dinner with those you cherish. Hospitality is among the main qualities of Asatru and the host is believed to be fortunate to have the privilege of hosting a dinner. Modern Asatru has an approach that is more relaxed towards hosting and realizes that hosting a banquet and hosting entertainment can be expensive, which is why they encourage collaboration. These kinds of gatherings remain enjoyable, and everyone is required to bring an item to table. This is a fantastic opportunity to exchange cultural food and sample something you not have had before.

Symbel

The symbel takes place following the meal and is comprised of drinking in a ritual. Mead, ale or wine is served in a cup or horn, and then transferred from person to. The host or Godi is the one responsible to pass the cup around and making sure everyone has a drink. Modern symbel rituals aim to strengthen the bonds of communities and unite people. Alcohol does not have to be present however, you can choose to use sparkling juice or sparkling water instead. Certain standards are set for the symbel, as well as drunkenness and bad behaviour are not allowed.

The basic rituals can be modified to accommodate more formal celebrations such as funerals, weddings and blessings, or other celebrations.

Chapter 7: What to Do To work with the Deities

Asatru is a religion that is polytheistic due to the fact that it has many gods. Pagan and heathenism are also polytheistic, meaning that multiple gods are involved. As we've already mentioned, Asatru doesn't have strict guidelines and texts to follow however, it does allow followers to explore their own ways of interacting with gods as well as the spirits. Asatru gods are considered to be individuals with their own unique personalities and characteristics.

The process of establishing a relationship with a god needs to be considered with care since they're as complex as relationships that we have in our daily lives. Asatru connections do not adhere to the same guidelines that they do in Western religions. In Christianity worshipers are required to see God as the ultimate standard to be able to live up to. The essence principle of Christianity is to worship the God of heaven and earth. In Norse pagan religions and Asatru the gods are more accessible and reflect both the good and bad of human behaviour.

How to Identify a Healthy Deity Relationship

What kind of relationships do exist in your daily life? The dynamic between a teacher and student as well as a parent and child deep and intimate friendships, superficial acquaintances, and lovers or partners. Our lives are full of problematic and healthy relationships. We all learn through our relationships and the relationships they foster.

The relationship between gods and deities is no different, and should be characterized with the help of the following guidelines

* Mutual agreement

* Communication is clear

* Respect for each other

* Implications of boundaries

* Communication is clear

The signs of unhealthy relationships are detected by

* Controlling actions

* Overstepping boundaries

* Pressure tactics

* Bullying

* Manipulative behavior

What to Expect When Engaging with Deities

It Requires Commitment

The deities are here and you're in this world wanting to be connected with them. So why you aren't seeing it happen? Are you putting the effort into it? Conducting research about your god or group, employing appropriate tools to form a magical connection, and enhancing your Clair senses will aid in forming relationships. There will be instances where you'll be hit and miss and you'll end up disappointed. Overcome that disappointment, and you'll emerge stronger.

The relationship exists between two Parties

If you have a relationship with the divinities, it's an extremely personal experience. Don't divulge your experiences unless you believe in the third person. Your family members and close family members will be able to understand that you prefer to remain private about your relationship and do not want to divulge information. No one should allow anyone to influence with your relationship and make judgments.

You Can Both Say No

Gods and mortals both have the freedom of choice They are not required to establish friendships if they don't wish to. Gods aren't expected to stand at your call since they are able to make choices just as you can.

You May Not Get On

If the god you select to worship appears to be to be a perfect relationship on paper, it's possible that you may alter your mind. Incompatibility can happen just as it happens in relationships, and it's fine. If you're not on the same mindset It could be a sign that you should have to separate or reconsider your relationship.

How to Identify a God Who is Trying to connect with You

The key is knowing when something isn't an unintentional coincidence, and could be an indication of the Gods. Everyone has unanswered dreams or omens, or experiences that seem strange. To determine if it's something more spiritual? Use the principle of Three. That means that if you see one sign that's not a coincidence, two of them are evidence or information, and the third is proof that Gods are communicating to you.

One aspect to think about can be confirmation bias. Humans are able to find proof to justify their beliefs even when the evidence isn't present. Be truthful with yourself and base your opinions on evidence instead of seeing results which aren't real. There's no harm in being optimistic but do not let it cloud your judgment.

Signs to Watch Out For

Omens

Omens are a symbol in the real world that originates in spiritual sources. Omens are mistakenly interpreted as a sign of a catastrophe, but it's simply a symbol in its most basic shape. The gods send you omens that are related to their connections. Odin has two ravens, Loki also has a fox and the other gods also are associated with specific significations. The way to interpret them is your choice. They are often associated with an "gut feeling," that sensation that something strange is occurring.

Dreams

Norse folk believed that dreams could be powerful, but they also recognized the distinction between meaningful visions and the random. They understood that dreams could be random in a variety of ways, and they even were given the name "draumskrok," which means "dream nonsense." It was believed by them that their destiny was already written out and that their destiny would be projected to them through dreams.

Deities can appear in a variety of shapes in dreams, and they transmit messages that may be specific or delivered to make the person receiving the message feel safe and secure in their presence. In Norse times, seers were used to interpret dreams and relay details. They may contain specific knowledge made to help the person dreaming to overcome difficulties or find hidden objects or even people.

If they were in the mood to dreams, Norse men and women used a variety of methods to incite them. They would lay down on graves or animal hides to indicate their willingness to communicate. Modern techniques are available to induce a kind of dreaming known as lucid dreaming. It means that you know that you're dreaming and you are in control of your surroundings and will be able to be able to recall the details at the time of awakening.

Your subconscious mind functions as an enormous database which contains all the details of every experience you've experienced even if you do not recall the details. It is possible to access this database any time you wish when you're in lucid dreams and the gods can help you create pictures, experiences and messages that they wish to communicate.

What Your Dreams Mean

What do you think about your fantasies? Do you consider them important in your life, or do believe they are just a flimsy image from your mind? If you're working with divinities, your dreams become a larger part of your nocturnal thoughts and you'll be able to discern their meaning as well as the meanings they carry.

There aren't any hard or fast answers, but the meanings given below will assist you in understanding how you are feeling and the messages divinities are telling you.

Dream Symbols and Their Meaning

1. Animals symbolize your connection to the natural world and the primordial part of your mental psyche. Are you in denial of your own emotions and hiding your personality? Release yourself and become the person you are supposed to be.

2. Being chased is a normal aspect of dreams, and it indicates that you are feeling threatened. Think about who or what is following you in order to identify the actual dangers you could confront in your life.

3. Exams or tests are a sign that you must evaluate your own. The gods are encouraging you to look at your own life and determine whether you need to make changes.

4. It is also a frequent sensation in dreams. It is a sign of anxiety that has lost control. Be aware of the aspects of your life which could be spiraling out of control.

5. The loss of a friend or loved one doesn't mean an indication or indication that they'll pass away in the physical world It's a sign of your relationships shifting. It may be the right time to reconsider and take difficult choices.

6. Hair symbolizes sexuality and sex. If you imagine that you're a hairy person and it's in excess and you're not satisfied, you're experiencing a healthy sexual desire. However, fantasies of being bald or shaving your head are a sign of the

opposite. Pay focus on your diet and overall health to boost your sexual desire.

7. Houses are significant dream symbols since they represent your inner psyche. Each floor and space is a repository of your emotions as well as memories. The gods are encouraging you to make use of them to remind you of what's important.

8. Babies and infants signify that you need to make a fresh beginning. It could be children, or it could mean that the gods feel that you are trapped in your current situation and require to think about a new direction.

9. The idea of killing yourself in dreams might seem like a lot but it's not an indication that you're a serial killer in the closet. It is a sign of your desire to "kill" certain parts of you. Get rid of bad mental habits or negative connections and you will become more positive.

10. A missed flight or meeting can cause you to be disappointed by missed opportunities. The gods are encouraging you to take advantage of opportunities whenever you have the chance. Don't be afraid of making the big decisions and make a risk.

11. The word "money" doesn't mean that it is a determinant of financial issues. In the dream, it symbolizes self-worth. If you think about it, you're giving it away. You let someone lower your self-worth. You have to recover it. If you imagine exchanging money, this is a sign of the beginning of a new phase within your personal life.

12. Mountains are the symbol for obstacles. If you imagine you're gazing at the views from the top of the mountain, it's an indication that you're successful and have achieved your goals. If you're stuck in the middle on the mountain gods are

telling you to set new goals and conquer the obstacles that are holding you back.

13. The idea of nakedness is common in dreams. It symbolizes your inner being getting visible before the public. If you have a dream that you're unattended at the office, you have to strengthen your relationships with those who you are working with. It also indicates the need to be acknowledged for both professional and social situations.

14. Televisions and other media devices are a sign of a desire to communicate. Make use of the chance to ask questions and observe what happens. You might be surprised by the outcome.

15. Schools are usually depicted in your dreams, and might be a sign that you're called back in time to simpler days. They also symbolize the need to be educated and knowledge, and the gods are

encouraging you to start new endeavors and to learn essential life lessons.

16. Sexuality and intimacy aren't always as simple as they seem. It is possible that you are seeking the intimacy that sex can bring but it could indicate that you should unify your feelings and your actions in order to increase your personal development.

17. Teeth are frequent in dreams. If you imagine the teeth getting lost, it indicates you're afraid of becoming old. Stressful situations can cause the same dreams.

18. Being trapped underground or in an area that is small is a sign that you're stuck. The gods have a message for you to get out and get out of you "safe space" to make sure that you are getting the best out of life.

19. The automobile is a symbol of the control you have in your personal life. Are

you driving or are you merely being a passenger? If your car is in a state of chaos it means that you are getting lost in your life.

20. The subconscious mind is represented by water. When the waters are calm then you are in control. But If the water appears to be choppy or cloudy, you're being told to get involved and grab hold of it.

How to Make Your Dreams More Lucid

There are a variety of methods for triggering lucid dreaming Some are more powerful than others. For beginners, it is recommended to start by using natural ingredients that yield a mild result before attempting more intense methods.

Vitamin B6

It is crucial to know how food choices influence your spitting and the most important component that is responsible for this happens to be vitamin B6. When you consume a supplement of 100mg 2 hours prior to bedtime you'll have more intense dreams. There aren't any products that provide B6 in the quantity you require, therefore taking a supplement is the sole method to boost your levels.

Tryptophan

Vitamin B6 helps your tryptophan in order to create serotonin, which makes your sleeping patterns and experiences more well-balanced. It can help with insomnia and encourages healthy sleep, which means you'll have more time to enjoy your dreams, and then remember them when you wake up in the morning.

Take these tryptophan-rich meals to increase the intensity of your dreams

* Chicken offers .10g per 1 ounce

* Turkey meat is priced at .09 per ounce

* Tuna fish has 0.09 per ounce

Organic lamb weighs 0.08 per 1 ounce

* Salmon costs 0.08 per 1 ounce

* Cod is 0.07 per 1 ounce

* Kidney beans contain 0.18 per cup.

* Cheese is 0.09 per one ounce

* Tofu is 0.03 per 1 ounce

Divination

Divination tools can be a wonderful method to communicate with deities. They provide a variety of ways of communicating and receiving information. There are a variety of methods to communicate using divination, for instance:

Dice Divination

Astrogalomancy sets date to 5 000 years ago in what is now Iran. Four-sided dice were popular in Roman times. They were known as "tali" and were numbered 1,3,4 and 6. The game was played with four dice at the same time The most flimsiest throw was four one's. Modern dice come with six sides, and are usually utilized in conjunction with circles. Draw roughly a 20cm circle, and then take three dice with six sides. Some players believe that only the dice inside the circle are relevant, and others believe that dice which are outside of the circle are crucial. Roll the dice to see what they mean.

A dice that is outside the circle indicates that arguments will be coming your way

Two dice outside can lead to problems and disruptions

Three dice on the table can are a sign of luck and your dreams are likely to come true

If the dice fall on top of one another it means that a present is coming your way

Add the dice numbers that are inside the circle. Use Table below in order to determine the significance.

One Family problems are coming to an end

TWO Look at the difficult situations you face; they might not be as straightforward as you think.

Three pleasant surprises are on the way your way

Four You're about to receive an unpleasant surprise or a heated argument

Five Things to look forward to: a new friendship strangers may surprise you.

Six friends may solicit a favor or you could experience an loss

Seven Someone has been telling falsehoods and gossip about you, however there could be a potential for a new relationship.

Eighth, slow down and reflect on your actions. You could be gifted with a present

Nine You'll be successful in your relationship as well as your love life will blossom

Ten A time of fresh beginnings and success, you'll participate in legal proceedings

Eleven You'll experience an unintentionally painful, short-term illness and separation from someone could cause you to feel sorrowful

TWELVE Expect a substantial amount of money. Seek legal advice and wait for a response

THIRTEEN You're about go through a time of sorrow Do not lose hope or get caught up in self-pity

Fourteen new friends can bring joy and excitement Expect to be greeted with new love and support from friends

For the next FIFTEEN, beware of fake friends and beware of getting caught up in the crossfire of others. Focus on your current tasks instead of starting new ones

SIXTEEN You'll take one trip that is short, but it will yield a profit and be entertaining

SEVENTEEN Listen to others particularly those who are located far away, and be ready to alter your plans

EIGHTEEN Happiness, success and financial luck will be your through your

161

If you're not keen to play with dice, check out the online divination websites that make use of dice to reveal your destiny

Tarot

The cards are powerful divination tools, and they could be read out by Tarot card readers and you may also try to interpret them yourself. Keep in mind that the cards have basic meanings, but they may be read in different ways depending on the question you're asking. Do not be afraid to experiment, but keep in mind that tarot cards can assist you in communicating with the gods, and may also have specific messages that they have to transmit. You might need to utilize several methods to obtain an accurate reading.

Cartomancy

This alternative divination method makes use of normal playing cards, not the tarot. Certain people feel more comfortable using regular playing cards than some of the spiritual imagery found on the cards of tarot. The origins of cartomancy are not clear, however many nations and cultures have been practicing it since the 14th century. There is speculation that Napoleon often sought out cartomancers in order to help predict his success and defeats.

The story of the past may be unclear however the power of the card is widely recognized and various cultures utilize cards to connect to spirits and to receive messages from them. Each deck is unique and has its own meaning to you, so take note of the questions you'd like to know and the meaning you're expecting from the interpretations you receive when selecting the cards you'll use.

Rune Readings

The runes played a significant role to the Norse gods, and Odin particularly believed in their prophetic qualities. There are numerous rune sets with instructions and interpretations. They come in wood as well as stone and typically come with a specially white cloth that you can cast the runes upon.

You can create your own runes as the most affordable option. this allows you to make connections on a deeper level to your set. Make sure to use smooth materials that will not harm your hands while reading. Wood, stone or crystal runes work great as do more natural stones that are shaped or pebbles.

The reading should take place in a peaceful location with a view of north to allow you to connect completely to Gods of the Norse gods. This can increase the effectiveness that the reader has and help make your messages more clear. Select a time that best suits your current energy level for casting your Runes. Some prefer casting at midnight, during the witching hour, and some believe that the sun offers the most cleansing energy. Your choice is up to you and there aren't any rules about what is the ideal time to cast.

When casting your runes, focus on specific questions. They could include as general as "What do I expect in the future" or more specific, such as "will I be able to pass the exam I'm taking next week?" and the responses will answer the question. Shuffle the runes on their sides and read three of them for a quick reading, as well as five for more specific answer.

The first rune should be placed on the right side, the second one to the left and the final one in the middle. If you're choosing five runes, put your first rune in the middle and create an arc around it, joining the remaining four. You can also scatter nine runes to gain an understanding and make an unpredictably shaped shape. In the event that you're blessed with three of them think of them as the past, present and future. The others will represent their significance based on the place they are.

Reading the Rune is a private experience that will be influenced by the gods you worship. It is possible to ask questions on various subjects and your responses will be corresponding to them based on the interpretation you make. Inquiring for assistance from divinities will determine how successful your interpretations are and affect the results. Select your gods carefully and be sure to prove that your intention is genuine.

Magic Basics

Utilizing Norse divination and magic is generally safe, however you must make sure you are taking basic precautions to protect yourself. As with the natural world there are dangerous elements and you must make sure you are prepared. If you've heard stories about people summoning spirits of evil using divination methods, they're likely to be rookies who make errors that aren't so obvious. It's not like you live your life without taking care and precautions, so why avoid them when it comes to spiritual work?

Cleanse Your Area

Your home must be a secure space where you can do your job. Be sure that it's clean physically and free of any negative energy. Utilize sage or other healing smoke to clear any energy which could interfere with the magic of your mind. Music and bells will clean your space and help create a positive place.

Grounding Yourself

You need to be in a good state of mind to be able to absorb the messages you're likely to receive. So focusing on your own wellbeing will ensure that you're in the best mental state. Make sure your mind is free of thoughts that could hinder your connection and create a blank space for the messages you'll receive.

Basic Grounding Techniques

Focusing

Choose an object you wish to draw your attention and concentrate your attention completely. Keep your breath in for 20 minutes, and let all other objects in your blur away. Focus on the object you have chosen and let your mind go completely.

Body Scan

Place yourself in the chair and keep your attention inwards. Imagine your breath entering and out of your body as visible gas. Then, focus on the areas of your body in the chair. What are they feeling like? Do you feel the soil under your feet? Does it feel solid is it a feeling of loose? Then, focus on those organs in your body. Feel your heart beat and visualize your mind clearing out and opening up to receive your messages.

Make a Note of External Stimuli

Then, in the same spot you can switch your focus to the space that you are in. What is the temperature? What is the shape of the space? Are there fragrances or hear any sound?

These exercises will help you learn how to pay attention and comprehend what's taking place inside your body and outside. Take note of the scents and textures, the temperatures and taste as you consume food. Pay attention to music and focus on the arrangement of what you hear. Find the instruments that you are interested in and the notes they're playing.

If you are able to begin living an enlightened lifestyle and become more mindful, you will begin to are more content with simple pleasures.

Origins and History of Asatru

Asatru is a pagan modern religion that began in the 20th century, however it wasn't until later that it gained recognition from Scandinavian governments. In 1972 In 1972, the Icelandic religious group, Asatruarfelagid (Asatru Fellowship) was founded. Within a year the organization was granted the status of a legally recognized religious institution. While the faith appears to be new developed, it is roots in Germanic religions that predated Christianity. The more appropriate term to describe Asatru could be "a reconstruction." Asatru is an offshoot of one of the many religions that existed in Scandinavia as well as in the Netherlands, France, England and other parts of Northern Europe before the arrival of Christianity. That is it's not necessarily a brand new religion but can be described as a revival older customs.

The word "asatru" in Ancient Norse, Asatru means "belief in the Aesir." The Aesir is one of the Norse Gods. Since the religion was practiced in such a vast area it was given numerous names. Vanatru, Forn Sed, Vor Sir, Forn Sir, Odinism, Wodenism, Nordisk Sed, and more. In English it is referred to in the English language as Norse and Germanic Heathenism. It is also known as Neo-paganism, it is not the case for the followers, who are known in the Asatruar.

The basis of Asatru is in various Norse myths that were recorded in the earliest scripts, particularly those of the Poetic or Prose Eddas. The customs, rituals, as well as values were discussed and described in sagas as well as the surviving texts. Be aware that the Asatruar do not necessarily believe in myths being historically accurate nor do they adhere to the literal implementation of old rituals such as blood sacrifices. But, they believe in the principles and ways of living that myths and rituals were a representation of. But, the subject is more complex than the above.

Originating as a folk faith, Norse paganism was a long trek to spread across Northern Europe. In addition, the religion was also threatened by the rise of expanding empires. Because of the threat of prosecution the religion went from being a religion with huge popularity to a largely obscure religion. In the end, Norse paganism reached a point at which it was totally wiped out. It was then that the Asatru religion was rebuilt until it took on the form it is today. It is possible to comprehend that by looking back to the beginnings of the Old Norse religion, which gave the seeds for Asatru.

Germanic Religion Pre-Christianity

In the Proto-Norse period, which lasted from the 2nd to the 8th century up to the 12th century during which The Old Norse religion thrived. It was a major in the political arena for a lengthy period of time, before it became replaced with Christianity and then took over the political and social arenas. In its heyday time, this Old Norse religion made its journey across the country mostly through word-of-mouth which resulted in the development of many mythological variations. Much like Snorri Sturluson's Poetic Edda and Prose Edda and Prose Edda, the Germanic texts were only discovered in the first half of the 13th century. These were literary texts historians wrote and then compiled from various sources. As of today, they are the most reliable source of details on Norse mythology.

Main Elements

Whatever the distinction in the accounts, Germanic people had the same and almost unifying convictions. In the beginning the religion they practiced was polytheistic. This means they believe in more than one god and a god pantheon that according to Snorri was divided into two gods groups that were that of the Aesir and Vanir. In particular those who believed in the Aesir gods and goddesses were Odin, Thor, and Frigg. For those of the Vanir gods they comprised Njordr, Freyr, and Freyja and many more. After a brutal war that devastated the land of both the Aesir along with the Vanir and the Vanir, they decided to make peace as both were equally strong.

In addition to the main gods and goddesses, Old Norse myths told of supernatural gods and deities. The first were the ancient gods that were worshipped in specific areas. There were also supernatural creatures, such as the Norns. Similar to they are similar to Fates from Greek mythology The Norns are three female entities that influence Gods as well as mortals, and believed in the past that they held completely in control. Since the birth of Asatru, the magnitude of their influence was an issue of debate. Yet, they're thought to be in existence, sitting at the Well of Fate, drawing water and tending to The Yggdrasill (universal trees).

Vaettir, sometimes referred to as wights is another instance that supernatural creatures exist. They are the old-fashioned spirit of the earth and nature and are based on the notion that every tree or mountain, river, or mountain is possessed by the spirit of. The term however does not only refer to the nature spirits. It may also refer to giants, elves as well as dwarfs. Nature spirits were and are frequently respected for their power. Their fury at human trespasses against nature causes natural catastrophes. Their presence is thought to be the main reason for the variety of good emotions we feel when we are in the wilderness and within nature.

Creation was a fervently discussed topic within Norse mythology, and several accounts that explains how the universe began to form. The text of Snorri, Gylfaginning, explains that the universe was nothing more than an empty space in the beginning. In the void, emerged two worlds: the dark, cold and icy desert that is Niflheim and the burning inferno of Muspelheim, a flaming land which was ruled by giants. From Niflheim was an ice blanket, and from Muspelheim there was a lava river. Within the Ginnungagap void the rivers collided. The opposing elements collided. the scorching lava melting the ice and form water, which brought to life the very first signs of Ymir the huge. The same water also created the legendary cattle, Audumbla.

Audumbla had two roles to play in the creation process. One was feeding Ymir their milk. Second, she was taking a lick of the salt cubes falling down Niflheim. Within one cube was the very first person in the Aesir The dad, Buri. Buri later gave birth to Bor through an unknown process. Bor got married to Bestla (a giant's daughter of a giant) in the following years. Together they gave birth to Odin, Vili, and Ve who decided to kill Ymir when they became bored of his destructive behavior. The death of the giant brought the birth of the universe. After the giant's death and his blood gushed out like an endless flow. Odin along with his companions carried Ymir's body into Gingnungagap's center, then, they went on to build the universe. They created land using his body, brain clouds and mountains, as well as rocks from bones and teeth hair, and the water surface made from his blood. Midgard (earth) is made from Ymir's eyelashes and to ensure the safety of the land giants were created to live in their kingdom, Jotunheim. On Idavoll's plains Idavoll the gods met to form Asgard.

Another key element in the Old Norse religion is Yggdrasill the sacred tree of ash which sits at the heart of the universe as it connects all the realms in Norse Cosmology. The branches of the tree extended across the sky, joining the nine realms of Asgard (land that is the home of Aesir), Midgard (middle land), Niflheim (land of fog), Muspelheim (land of fire), Jotunheim (land of the giants), Vanaheim (Vanir land), Alfheim (elf land), Svartalfheim (land of the dark the elves) along with Helheim (land that is the burial site).

Three of the Yggdrasil's root systems are located ones: one is near one of the Well of Fate in Asgard which is where the gods get together to discuss the issues of the universe, another located in Jotunheim close to the source of Mimir and another located in Niflheim close to Hvergelmir's spring. Hvergelmir. With the help of the three main Norns The tree is able to flourish and bear its weight with the entire world and the creatures who live on the sacred tree. If it is not taken care of the tree is afflicted, and consequently, the whole world is affected. The moment the tree starts to shake It was believed to signify that it is the start of Ragnarok or the end of the days.

Ragnarok isn't just one event but a sequence of events that make up the end of the world. According to ancient texts the prophecy was that the realms of nine would be at war with one another in a the battle. The Midgard serpent will kill Thor The Thunderer. Gods and humans are set to die, realms will be destroyed and the moon and the sun as well. After all has been destroyed one man and a woman who sought refuge in Yggdrasil will emerge to repopulate the earth under a brand new sun. This is what Germanic people believed would happen at the end, however with regard to the Asatruar belief system, it has somewhat changed. Many people still accept the myth as factual While others recognize the significance of the symbolism, and believe in the fundamental truths and beliefs that are embodied in Ragnarok instead.

Apart from this huge knowledge of gods and their roots, Germanic people were worshippers of gods in many different forms than they could count. However, these traditions were not included in myths and poems. They were only mentioned in sagas . They traveled across the globe via words of mouth. As a folk religion Old Norse was mainly dependent on the understanding of the people about the practices, rituals and principles of worship. There was no one text which commanded the "correct" method of practicing the religion. This is the reason there are various variations of rituals for worship.

Temples and Statues

Before Christianity came to Scandinavian areas, a variety of Nordic altars, temples, and statues were in the vicinity. The worshippers and seekers would use statues to praise God and to ask for direction and safety. Contrary to most religions and societies, Nordic statues were divided into statues that had human-like characteristics and other comprised of wood staves with heads carved on top and a faint resemblance to the totems. In many cases, the gods were depicted alongside animals and symbols connected to them.

A tiny silver statue of Odin was found during excavations in Old Lejre. Old Lejre. The statue depicted him seated on a throne. To each side, were the ravens who served as his messengers, Huginn and Muninn. Today, it's difficult to find huge statues because none survived Christianization. The ones that survived were easy to conceal figurines and smaller statues, and amulets. One of the most popular design of amulets was that with the Hammer that was the symbol of Thor, Mjolnir, a symbol of protection. Others, that were not as explicit pagan, also resembled designs and ribbons that resembled Scandinavian style.

For temples, they were big barn-like structures in which worshipers were able to make offerings, drink mead and enjoy a meal in honour of gods. However, some research has revealed that temples were not exclusively intended for use for religious purposes. Festivals of religious significance included a lot of gatherings and tourists from different places to attend the celebrations. It was also an opportunity for vendors and farmers to market their products and products, which is why the Nordic religious celebration was typically more than a solely celebration of religion. But, it didn't mean that temples were ungoverned. Temples were usually enclosed by a border that designated the territory as holy soil , on which blood was not allowed to spill.

In the sense that Old Norse was a religion which was a great deal of a connection to the spirit of nature and the spirits of nature, sacrifices were not limited to statues and temples. In many instances it was customary to offer offerings in the form of fords, lakes,